Mutual Mentoring for Mid-Career Teachers

Mentoring is for teachers across the career span! In this helpful resource, authors Karen Weller Swanson and Micki M. Caskey show how mid-career mentoring can rejuvenate your joy of teaching, plan for career progressions, and build a healthy work-life balance.

The authors lay out a framework for mutual mentoring that uses a trekking metaphor and a choose-your-own-adventure style, which allows for individualized professional development focusing on topics most important to you. Through this approach, you will learn how to create a community of practice with other teachers, how to engage in dialogue about teaching and exchange ideas, methods for productively responding to challenges, and ideas for learning new skills and revising or abandoning practices. The authors also cover how to establish healthy boundaries, create a sustainable practice, and implement plans to achieve professional goals.

With this book, mid-career teachers will be able to thrive in a mentoring space that creates opportunities for them to embrace innovative and collaborative practices and explore their evolving personal and teacher identities.

Karen Weller Swanson, EdD, was a Professor of Curriculum and Instruction. She has mentored teachers in master's programs at George Mason University and the University of Nebraska. Karen was the Director of the Ph.D. in Curriculum and Instruction program at Mercer University. In this role she mentored doctoral students in research, writing, and career development. Karen has served on the board of the Association for Middle Level Education and as Chair of the Research Advisory Board and Editor of Research in Middle Level Online. Karen also serves on the board of the Colorado Association of Middle Level Education. She is currently an eighth-grade science teacher in Colorado.

Micki M. Caskey, PhD, is a Professor Emerita in the Department of Curriculum and Instruction in the College of Education at Portland State University. She specializes in mentoring teachers in professional practice, middle grades education, and doctoral education programs. She has experience as an associate dean for academic affairs, doctoral program director, writing coach, and teacher educator. She is a co-series editor of *The Handbook of Research in Middle Level Education* and *The Handbook of Resources in Middle Level Education*. Micki is a former middle school teacher who taught in urban settings for more than 20 years.

Mutual Mentoring for Mid-Career Teachers

Trekking with Colleagues for Joy and Growth

Karen Weller Swanson and Micki M. Caskey

Routledge
Taylor & Francis Group
NEW YORK AND LONDON

Designed cover image: Getty Images

First published 2026
by Routledge
605 Third Avenue, New York, NY 10158

and by Routledge
4 Park Square, Milton Park, Abingdon, Oxon, OX14 4RN

Routledge is an imprint of the Taylor & Francis Group, an informa business

© 2026 Karen Weller Swanson and Micki M. Caskey

The right of Karen Weller Swanson and Micki M. Caskey to be identified as authors of this work has been asserted in accordance with sections 77 and 78 of the Copyright, Designs and Patents Act 1988.

All rights reserved. No part of this book may be reprinted or reproduced or utilised in any form or by any electronic, mechanical, or other means, now known or hereafter invented, including photocopying and recording, or in any information storage or retrieval system, without permission in writing from the publishers.

For Product Safety Concerns and Information please contact our EU representative GPSR@taylorandfrancis.com. Taylor & Francis Verlag GmbH, Kaufingerstraße 24, 80331 München, Germany.

Trademark notice: Product or corporate names may be trademarks or registered trademarks, and are used only for identification and explanation without intent to infringe.

Library of Congress Cataloging-in-Publication Data
Names: Weller Swanson, Karen author | Caskey, Micki M. author
Title: Mutual mentoring for mid-career teachers: trekking with colleagues for joy and growth / Karen Weller Swanson and Micki M. Caskey.
Description: New York, NY: Routledge, 2026. | Includes bibliographical references.
Identifiers: LCCN 2025039958 (print) | LCCN 2025039959 (ebook) |
ISBN 9781032957289 hardback | ISBN 9781032957265 paperback | ISBN 9781003586241 ebook
Subjects: LCSH: Mentoring in education | Teachers—Professional relationships | Teacher effectiveness
Classification: LCC LB1731.4 .W42 2026 (print) | LCC LB1731.4 (ebook)
LC record available at https://lccn.loc.gov/2025039958
LC ebook record available at https://lccn.loc.gov/2025039959

ISBN: 978-1-032-95728-9 (hbk)
ISBN: 978-1-032-95726-5 (pbk)
ISBN: 978-1-003-58624-1 (ebk)

DOI: 10.4324/9781003586241

Typeset in Palatino
by codeMantra

Dedication

To our mentors, our colleagues, and our families who walked beside us on our personal and professional adventures.

To our many teacher-friends who trekked with us as we climbed over boulders, traveled new terrain, reached new heights, and celebrated our successes.

Contents

Prologue	1
Adventure Awaits	1
What Is the Purpose of the Book?	2
Why Write a Book about Teacher-Friends?	3
Mid-Career Teacher Retention and Renewal	6
The Trekking Metaphor	7
How Can You Use This Book?	8
About the Authors	11
Conclusion	13
References	13
Part 1: Wandering	**17**
1 Mutual Mentoring: Teacher-Friends	19
Mutually Beneficial	19
Critical Thinking	21
Choosing a Teacher-Friend	24
Teaching Phases	26
Teacher Identity	27
Hydration Station	30
Trail Talks	30
Keeping a Journal	30
Conclusion	31
References	32
2 Self-Directed Learning: Trekking with a Partner or Solo	35
Self-Directed Learning	36
Teacher-Friends	39
Gear to Support Self-Directed Learning	46
Conclusion	49
References	49
3 Communication: Dialogue, Conversation, and Good Talk	52
Dialogue	53
Conversation	58
Good Talk	60

	Connecting to Practice	63
	Conclusion	65
	References	66
4	**Practice: Going Deeper and Moving Forward**	**69**
	Key Features of Teacher Practice	70
	Engaging in Practice	73
	Supporting Practice through Dialogue	77
	Conclusion	82
	References	82
Part 2: Exploring		**87**
5	**Resilience, Transformative Learning, and Teacher Identity**	**89**
	Resilience	90
	Transformative Learning	94
	Teacher Identity	98
	Conclusion	99
	References	101
6	**Packing, Unpacking, and Repacking**	**103**
	Reflective Practice: Talking and Writing to Learn	104
	What to Pack, Unpack, and Repack	107
	Using Critical Reflection to Unpack Practice	109
	Engaging in Practice	114
	Conclusion	115
	References	117
7	**Critical Thinking, Passion, and Work-Life Balance**	**119**
	Critical Thinking	120
	Passion, Exhaustion, and Recovery	122
	Exploring Work-Life Balance	128
	Conclusion	132
	References	133
Part 3: Venturing		**137**
8	**Preparing for an Adventure**	**139**
	Adventure	139
	Possible Destinations	140
	Trekking Gear: Having the Right Stuff	143

	What We Bring in Our Backpack	145
	Conclusion	150
	References	150
9	**On Our Way**	**151**
	Keep Moving	152
	Resting Is Not Quitting	157
	Sharing Your Trek	158
	Conclusion	159
	References	160
10	**Looking Back, Looking Ahead**	**161**
	Looking Back: Our Big Ideas	162
	Looking Ahead: Our Beliefs	167
	Beliefs about Teaching	168
	Conclusion	169
	References	170

Epilogue: Micki and Karen's Trekking Adventure — 171

Prologue

Adventure Awaits

Welcome to mid-career teacher mentoring. This book evolved from a long friendship between us. We shared a teaching path that intersected in multiple ways over many years. Ironically, we have never lived in the same state or worked in the same building. We both began our teaching careers as middle school teachers. Micki started in Florida, and Karen started in Arizona. We joined the Association for Middle Level Education early in our careers. We were lucky enough to be actively engaged in that organization throughout our careers. This is where we met and joined talents to work together. Now we have brought our passion for teaching and teachers together in this book. In other words, we decided to be teacher-friends years ago.

We both will retire from the teaching profession. We have experienced the challenges teachers face as the political climate, financial constraints, and parenting trends change over many decades. The current teaching environment is stressful; our goal in writing this book is to provide mid-career teachers, like ourselves, with some tools to manage the changes, care for ourselves, and sustain the joy of teaching.

Persistent Challenges

Many say teaching is rewarding and retire at 30 years—full of joy. Others leave after five years or less, frustrated with the disconnect between their expectations and the reality of the job. How do you make sense of this mixed reality associated with teaching as a career choice? We note that several school and societal factors create a negative work environment. In a study by

Fogelgarn and Burns (2020), six concerns were consistent across the teachers in the study:

1. Unsupportive school management
2. Crowded curriculum
3. Systemic compliance
4. Societal negativity
5. Threats to teacher well-being and
6. Negative collegial impacts

Fogelgarn and Burns concluded that it was remarkable that teachers in the study were able to be resilient and to sustain their passion through effective practice. If the list of factors that undermine teacher passion continues as a professional liability, it is more important than ever to help mid-career teachers understand that negative factors exist and how to develop boundaries to mitigate them.

While mentoring programs for induction and early career teachers are common, we offer an approach that creates the space for the necessary conversations for those who are past induction yet a long way from retirement. Our goal is to address mindset in terms of personal goals and professional possibilities through a focus on dialogue and practice.

In this prologue, we describe the who (teachers with 5–20 years of teaching experience), what (engaging in productive dialogue and practice about teaching), and why (to align personal and professional expectations and goal setting to maintain a growth mindset), as well as how to use this book. We end with our own journey about our relevant experience and what has impacted our individual and collective treks in education.

What Is the Purpose of the Book?

The purpose of this book is to provide a practical approach for mentoring teachers who are mid-career (i.e., 5–20 years) and are grappling with the question: "Is it worth staying?" Because many mid-career teachers are leaving the profession, an intentional mentoring approach is needed to encourage teacher retention. We designed this book to reignite a positive and well-reasoned conversation about teaching and professional growth.

Mutual mentoring is a process of deconstructing barriers that teachers face, which prevent them from having an authentic connection with their teaching practice. We regard teaching as a professional practice. Teachers discuss classroom issues every day with their peers. Our goal is to provide a guide to those conversations and raise the value of those conversations to the level of individualized professional development.

Everyone can benefit from mentoring, but it is not a one-size-fits-all fix. We believe that a robust mutual mentoring approach between two mid-career teachers can rejuvenate the joy of teaching. A significant number of teachers quit before year five (Sims & Jerrim, 2020), and for those in the middle grades that number of leavers is even higher (Nguyen et al., 2020).

Why Write a Book about Teacher-Friends?

We are experienced teachers. We have tremendous respect and empathy for the demands of teaching, and we want to support educators. As ideas swirled in and among our conversations with each other and our peers, we decided to share what we know about current teaching demands, teacher retention and shortages, the long road in choosing to stay in the profession, and the many joys of the art of teaching.

Given our experiences as practitioners, we repeatedly saw a gap in the literature regarding mentoring approaches for experienced teachers. After ruminating on this void, we decided on a course of action to expand our conversations. We felt we could create a wider conversation about mentoring experienced teachers by writing about individualized professional development that elevated teachers' conversations and practice.

Teacher retention is a complex issue. We have concerns that those gifted and prepared to teach are unable to see themselves retired from a profession that they love. However, school bureaucracy sometimes compels them to consider leaving a school or leaving the profession. We believe that good teachers can also be good mentors for their mid-career peers. Leveling up from hallway or professional learning community conversations to an intentional and organized process to mentor and be mentored can positively acknowledge the mental, emotional, and physical aspects of a job that many times go unnoticed.

Meaningful teacher mentoring programs that focus on professional growth can help experienced teachers thrive, feel empowered, and make a difference in students' lives. We list research that illustrates the consequences of the disconnect when mid-career teachers do not receive appropriate professional development:

- In a 2022 survey of 831 teachers, Phi Delta Kappa found "more than three-fourths (76.4%) of teachers surveyed considered leaving their position during the 2021-22 school year" (Marshall et al., 2022, p. 8).
- Teachers reported that the impetus for considering a change was exhaustion, workload, student behavior, and pay (Marshall et al., 2022).
- Years of teaching experience does not indicate that teachers do not need specialized professional development (Eros, 2011).
- Ronfeldt et al. (2013) reported that teacher turnover negatively affects student achievement.
- Mid-career teachers need prompts and time to reflect, set goals, and evaluate their efficacy and effectiveness (Bressman et al., 2018).

The issues that teachers encounter daily and the negative impact of teachers leaving on student achievement are central to why we are writing this book. We believe that increased student achievement and increased teacher efficacy and engagement can and should be complimentary. Based on 40 years of research, Zee and Koomen (2016) explained that teacher burnout is directly connected to lower levels of efficacy, which is defined as a teacher's perceptions of their ability to achieve desired outcomes.

We have written articles, chapters, and books throughout our career. We have taught hundreds of teacher candidates and advised hundreds of teachers pursuing their master's and doctoral degrees. As a result, we have read broadly in educational research and literature about teacher development. As you read this book we introduce you to a few of our favorite people. We hope you enjoy them as much as we do. They have stretched our thinking and validated our experience. Parker Palmer is one of those authors. Palmer (1998) identified issues related to teacher retention 25 years ago, asserting:

> *In our rush to reform education, we have forgotten a simple truth: reform will never be achieved by renewing appropriations, restructuring schools, rewriting curricula, and revising texts if we continue to demean and dishearten the human resource called the teacher on whom so much depends. Teachers must be better compensated, freed from bureaucratic harassment, given a role in academic governance, and provided with the best possible methods and materials. But none of that will transform education if we fail to cherish—and challenge—the human heart that is the source of good teaching.*
>
> (p. 3)

We echo his sentiment that structure and skill are essential to effective teaching, but it is the heart of a teacher that sustains a long career.

The list of demands on teachers is palatable in schools and teacher conversations. We suggest that elevating that conversation to empower teachers in substantive ways that increase efficacy is the end goal for mentoring mid-career teachers. Conversations between teachers can include venting frustrations about problems that seem to be unsolvable. The result may ultimately lead to teachers deciding to leave the profession. We coin the word "teacher-friend" which is a relationship that supports growth and sharing between skilled, trusted colleagues. We contend that teacher-friend mentoring can build individuals' skills to approach and solve problems within their own classroom.

The increasing demands of teaching compelled us to develop a framework for teacher-friend mentorship. We defined a teacher-friend as a chosen colleague who shares common interests, challenges, dreams, and goals. We framed teacher-friend mentoring as an enduring relationship that traverses personal and professional life. The purpose of this teacher-friend mentoring approach is to tap into the support experienced teachers can provide for one another. In the next section, we summarize the research on teacher retention and categorize the information into *why teachers stay* and *why teachers leave* the profession.

Mid-Career Teacher Retention

Mid-career teacher retention has become an increasingly urgent issue. In fact, researchers have identified the high rate of teacher turnover overall as one of the most "pressing challenges facing the American public education system" (Gimbert & Kapa, 2022, p. 228). More than a decade ago, Ingersoll et al. (2014) found a downward trend in mid-career teacher retention. The high rate of teacher turnover has not abated (Ingersoll et al., 2022).

Recent reports about mid-career teacher retention revealed facts about why teachers stay in the profession or at their schools.

- ◆ A teacher's level of satisfaction with workplace conditions that directly impact their teaching is the most important factor in mid-career teacher retention (Gimbert & Kapa, 2022).
- ◆ Teachers in secondary school settings are more likely to stay in the profession than their peers in elementary schools (Gimbert & Kapa, 2022).
- ◆ Suburban mid-career teachers are more likely to express a desire to remain in the profession than teachers in urban and rural settings (Gimbert & Kapa, 2022).
- ◆ Teachers who have good professional development are more likely to stay in the profession (Nguyen et al., 2020).

- Positive school climate and attitudinal factors are related to mid-career teachers' intention to remain in the profession (Gimbert & Kapa, 2022).
- Teachers are more likely to remain in teaching when they can contribute to school policy decisions (Gimbert & Kapa, 2022).

Research also identified why teachers leave the profession or their schools.

- Many mid-career teachers (50%) have expressed an intention to leave the teaching profession (Gimbert & Kapa, 2022).
- Most teachers who leave the teaching profession are leaving before retirement (Ingersoll & Tran, 2023).
- Teachers in middle school settings are more likely to leave the teaching profession than elementary school teachers (Nguyen et al., 2020).
- Teachers leave their occupation at higher rates than others (e.g., nurses, engineers, lawyers, police officers) (Ingersoll et al., 2022).
- Teacher turnover rates are higher among minority and teachers of color than White, non-Hispanic teachers (Ingersoll et al., 2022).
- STEM and special education teachers have higher turnover rates than other content area teachers (Nguyen et al., 2020).
- Teachers are more likely to leave schools with less favorable working conditions related to disciplinary problems, facilities, or work assignments (Nguyen et al., 2020).
- Teachers cite dissatisfaction with school management, accountability and testing requirements, and school decision-making policies as reasons for leaving the profession (Ingersoll et al., 2022).

Mid-Career Teacher Retention and Renewal

Mentoring is a long-standing approach to onboarding and supporting new teachers entering the teaching profession. Early career mentoring prompts improvements in classroom practices (Mathur et al., 2013; Sowell, 2017) and teacher retention (Maready et al., 2021; Morettini, 2016; Renbarger & Davis, 2019). Mentoring among experienced mid-career teachers can lead to positive outcomes. Mid-career teachers include teachers with 5–20+ years of teaching experience. During mid-career, teachers "grow in confidence and have a sense of comfort about their approaches to teaching and learning. Their attention shifts from self to their students, and they explore ways to enrich their teaching skills and improve student's learning experience" (Bressman et al., 2018, p. 164). Mentoring mid-career teachers can prevent the unnecessary loss of teacher experience and expertise.

While early career teachers benefit from learning on their own or from other teachers, mid-career teachers gain a greater sense of autonomy or agency in selecting their own professional development (Brunetti & Marston, 2018). Mentoring is an effective way to:

- improve teachers' confidence in taking risks and their ability to make a difference (Cordingley & Buckler, 2012);
- reduce or eliminate teacher burnout (Irby et al., 2020); and
- reduce teacher turnover (Nguyen et al., 2020).

Yet, mentoring needs to be meaningful and responsive to individual needs throughout teachers' careers as their needs and interests change over time.

Schools need to weave mentoring into the fabric of school structure (Heynoski et al., 2022). In a recent report of the Association of American School Personnel Administrators, Heynoski et al. (2022) discussed the national teacher shortage and identified five shifts for improving teacher recruitment and retention. These shifts included creating pathways to careers in education, providing educators with more resources, increasing educator pay, supporting employee wellness, and promoting the profession. The report also called out mentoring specifically and offers recommendations:

- Address the lack of resources and mentoring which affect teachers' working conditions.
- Provide mentoring, professional development, and networking opportunities for administrators who manage people so they can be effective mentors.
- Form a statewide network to connect experienced mentors with novice teachers and provide differentiated programming.
- Recruit diverse teachers and former teachers to be mentors.
- Create specific early mentoring for teachers of color.

We argue that mentoring can help stave off teachers leaving the profession and lead to greater teacher retention.

The Trekking Metaphor

We are both walkers, hikers, travelers, and ever so curious. We chose the trekking metaphor over hiking because in trekking you don't go back to where you started from; you end up somewhere new. This appeals to our sense of adventure and our personal goals to learn more, ask more questions, grapple with new ideas, and get out of town! In our trekking research we found an irreverent author who has made us laugh, think, and reflect with her refreshing take on walking in the outdoors. Diana Helmuth (2021) wrote *How to Suffer Outside. A Beginner's Guide to Hiking and Backpacking*. In the preface, she wrote:

> *Your desire to go into nature comes from the same part of you that wishes to be secure. It doesn't want to depend on others for self-assurance and approval. It doesn't want to be addicted to buzzing rectangles and 30-second videos and 280-character quips. It craves reflection and depth and connects with a more tangible, eternal whole. It wants to give you a minute to work out all the tangible crap in your brain that you've been avoiding.*
>
> (p. 12)

In essence, we find a strong parallel between Helmuth's characterization of the desire going into nature and our concept of mid-career teacher mentoring with individualized professional development. As you read our book, you will come across elements of trekking gear indicated by a picture that invite you to reflect, talk, listen, remove some heavy ideas that might weigh you down, or pick up some new ideas that can make your trip more enjoyable (see Table 0.1).

We weave these elements throughout the book. You may even add to the metaphor as you design and implement your own professional development adventure. We have enjoyed exploring ways to use this metaphor to sustain our interest in mutual mentoring, individualized professional development, self-directed learning, and mutual mentoring. We hope you do, too.

How Can You Use This Book?

You can read this book in a couple of ways. You can choose *your own adventure approach*, meaning that you could read the chapters in the order you wish. Start with a chapter that appeals to you or intrigues you. For instance, you can read Chapter 10 before you begin your adventure or after. Or you can choose a *sequential approach* by starting with Chapter 1 and proceeding through each chapter until you reach the end. Whatever approach you choose, we know that you can take away mentoring ideas to use in your own teaching practice.

Table 0.1 Trekking Gear Metaphor Key

Gear in Alphabetical Order	Symbolism
	• A backpack holds what we think we need to be successful on a trek. It might include extra water and food, band-aids, extra layers of clothes, and so on. • Our backpacks also hold our assumptions about ourselves, teaching, and the future. It holds our curriculum and our instructional strategies. It holds our hopes and our disappointments.
	• Boots represent our authentic self, our choices, and our comfort. • Boots symbolize the strength and readiness required to face challenges and navigate difficult terrain. Our boots show evidence of our previous trips through the wear and tear on the boots.
	• A camera represents a reflection of a single situation or moment. • A picture allows us to revisit a situation, notice the details, and fill in the blanks about what happened before and after the event.
	• A compass symbolizes guidance and direction. While the scenery of a trek may be beautiful, you may be off track for your destination. A compass helps you know when you are lost and how to get back on track. • A compass represents checking to see that we are on the correct path.
	• A journal represents time to reflect. Reflection can be a process captured in our journals as we look for reasons, patterns, or answers. • The journal symbol is an invitation to take out your journal and consider the prompts provided or to just free write.

	• A map represents our individualized professional development plan.
	• A map symbolizes your plan.
	  – What do you plan to do?
	  – What do you want to see along the way?
	  – How to determine if you are still on the right path?

	• A magnifying glass represents the examination of our assumptions.
	• A magnifying glass invites us to ask questions about our practice of:
	  – Our colleagues
	  – Our students
	  – Ourselves
	  – Theory and research

(Continued)

Gear in Alphabetical Order	Symbolism
(sunglasses)	• Sunglasses represent our perspectives, attitudes, and values we hold about teaching and learning. • Using sunglasses on a trek helps us focus on acknowledging our attitudes and values while being open to learning from each other.
(sunscreen)	• Sunscreen is a metaphor for personal and professional boundaries. • Using sunscreen can mitigate short-term and long-term consequences.
(trail)	• Trail Talks represent the conversations that inform our thinking. We prompt you with questions to have conversations about topics in each chapter. • Trail talks afford you time to consider new ideas and revisit familiar ideas.
(walking poles)	• Walking poles represent support, reliance, and balance. • Walking poles can provide aid—whether from within as inner strength or from others. They are a symbol of resilience and progress, even when movement is slow or uncertain.
(water bottle)	• Water refreshes our bodies and reinvigorates us when we are thirsty. • The water bottle represents a pause in each chapter to stop and consider recent research on a specific topic at each hydration station.

You can also use this book in a several ways.

1. It is well suited for *pair reading* between two or more experienced teachers—with alternating roles as mentor and mentee.
2. It also works well for larger groups of experienced teachers who share our belief that everyone can benefit from mentoring.
3. Teachers can use this book for their *staff book club*—reading and discussing the mentoring ideas at regular intervals.
4. Other teachers can use this book as they seek additional credentials or certificates in mentoring, teacher leadership, or educational leadership (principalship).
5. In addition, you can use this book to guide formal professional development within your school or school district. We encourage you to use this book in ways that work best for you.

About the Authors

We are not only lifelong teachers but lifelong learners as well. Writing this book required us to examine our assumptions and do research about national teaching trends and types of mentoring that would refresh and reimagine staying in teaching for the long run for those who may not have originally planned to stay.

We recognize the privilege and honor of having spent our careers in the company of teachers and students. Our experience leads us to the understanding that while newly minted teachers need mentoring to learn the craft, experienced teachers need renewal through conversations about the art of teaching, the goals to feel successful, and the community in which they practice.

Micki M. Caskey

As we delve into writing this book about mentoring, I find myself reflecting on my own experiences as both a mentee (protégé) and mentor. I acknowledge that, as a White woman, I enjoyed the benefits of being a member of the dominant culture and having mentors who looked like me. As a high school junior, they prompted me to seek early admission to Chatham College in Pittsburgh, where I earned my bachelor's degree. Having these strong women mentors, including my own mother, helped to shape my humanistic stance. Fresh out of college, I started teaching middle grades youth in Tampa, where most of my students were poor White, Black, and Brown youth. After witnessing staggering educational disparities and vast learning differences among my students, I realized that I needed to know more and pursued a master's degree and teaching credentials in special education. Throughout my teaching career, I have taught historically marginalized and underserved students. These students (and their families) became my mentors and helped to expand my worldview beyond didactic and hierarchical ways of teaching to embrace and enact more collaborative, responsive, invitational, and inclusive practices. During my years as a public-school teacher, I also learned to be a mentor for aspiring teachers and experienced teachers. Later, as a university professor, I continued to mentor teachers but also to teach and mentor doctoral students. Whether in my role as advisor, instructor, or writing coach, my focus has been supporting doctoral students from underrepresented groups—Black, Latino, Native American, and English language learners as they pursued their scholarly aims and chased their passions. I have continued to mentor doctoral students and faculty colleagues to reach their goals, who in turn guide my development as a mentor—learning and growing together.

Karen Weller Swanson

I have been a mentee and a mentor throughout my 35 years in teaching and teaching education. As a native Montanan, my early exposure to race and ethnicity was limited. However, I went to college and taught science and English as a Second Language in Flagstaff, Arizona, where I learned with and about the Navajo and Hopi people through teaching indigenous students. Our school and community were home to Spanish-speaking immigrants. Once I received my doctorate in Curriculum and Instruction, I moved to northern Virginia to work at George Mason University. While there I had the privilege of consulting for the Maya Angelo Public Charter School in Washington, DC. This school catered to Black students who needed an alternative setting and work skills. My time at MAPCS really helped me articulate the role that white privilege has played in my life. I began to work with teachers in their master's program to identify their privilege and better meet the needs of minority students in their classrooms. I then transitioned to Mercer University in Atlanta to direct a doctoral program in Curriculum and Instruction. It was here that I realized the real work of Black women in the program and the lack of mentoring for them at the university and at their schools. It is in Atlanta that I served on the board of Tapestry Public Charter School. This school was a 6–12 model that was designed for students with autism and neurotypical students. These experiences have led me to question the assumptions I have as a white woman and reflect on how to grant privilege to my colleagues and middle school students. I am currently teaching eighth-grade science in Colorado, which is a beautiful full circle in my career.

Conclusion

Mentoring is an ongoing process of finding a trusted colleague to talk, laugh, curse, dream, and hope with around teaching and life. We know mutually beneficial mentoring works because we have been trekking together for more than 20 years. Our goal is to provide a structure that makes mentoring worth your investment.

References

Bressman, S., Winter, J. S., & Efron, S. E. (2018). Next generation mentoring: Supporting teachers beyond induction. *Teaching and Teacher Education, 73*, 162–170. https://doi.org/10.1016/j.tate.2018.04.003

Brunetti, G. J., & Marston, S. H. (2018). A trajectory of teacher development in early and mid-career. *Teachers and Teaching, 24*(8), 874–892. https://doi.org/10.1080/13540602.2018.1490260

Cordingley, P., & Buckler, N. (2012). Mentoring and coaching for teachers' continuing professional development. In S. Fletcher, & C. Mullen (Eds.), *The SAGE handbook of mentoring and coaching in education* (pp. 215–227). SAGE Publications Ltd. https://doi.org/10.4135/9781446247549.n15

Eros, J. (2011). The career cycle and the second stage of teaching: Implications for policy and professional development. *Arts Education Policy Review, 112*(2), 65–70. https://doi.org/10.1080/10632913.2011.546683

Fogelgarn, R., & Burns, E. A. (2020). What constrains passionate teaching?: A heuristic exploration. *Issues in Educational Research, 30*(2), 493–511.

Gimbert, B. G., & Kapa, R. R. (2022). Mid-career teacher retention: Who intends to stay, where, and why? *Journal of Education Human Resources, 40*(2), 228–265. https://doi.org/10.3138/jehr-2020-0037

Helmuth, D. (2021). *How to suffer outside. A beginner's guide to hiking and backpacking.* Mountaineers Book.

Heynoski, K., Douglas-McNab, E., Khandaker, N., Tamang, T., & Howell, E. (2022). *Shortage to surplus: 5 shifts to address the national educator shortage*. American Association of School Personnel Administrators. https://assets.noviams.com/novi-file-uploads/aaspa/AASPA-5_Shifts_NESS_FINAL-ded1e783.pdf

Ingersoll, R. M., Merrill, L., & Stuckey, D. (2014). *Seven trends: The transformation of the teaching force*. CPRE Report #RR-80. Consortium for Policy Research in Education, University of Pennsylvania.

Ingersoll, R. M., Merrill, E., Stuckey, D., Collins, G., & Harrison, B. (2022). *Five trends shaping the teaching force*. National Association of State Boards of Education. https://nasbe.nyc3.digitaloceanspaces.com/2022/09/Ingersoll-Merrill-Stuckey-Collins-Harrison_Sept-2022-Standard.pdf

Ingersoll, R. M., & Tran, H. (2023). Teacher shortages and turnover in rural schools in the US: An organizational analysis. *Educational Administration Quarterly, 59*(2), 396–431. https://doi.org/10.1177/0013161X231159922

Irby, B. J., Abdelrahman, N., & Lara-Alecio, R. (2020). Mentoring across teacher career stages. *Oxford Research Encyclopedia of Education*. https://doi.org/10.1093/acrefore/9780190264093.013.624

Maready, B., Cheng, Q., & Bunch, D. (2021). Exploring mentoring practices contributing to new teacher retention: An analysis of the Beginning Teacher Longitudinal Study. *International Journal of Evidence Based Coaching and Mentoring, 19*(2), 88–99. https://doi.org/10.24384/rgm9-sa56

Marshall, D. T., Pressley, T., Neugebauer, N. M., & Shannon, D. M. (2022). Why teachers are leaving and what we can do about it. *Phi Delta Kappan, 104*(1), 6–11. https://doi.org/10.1177/00317217221123642

Mathur, S. R., Gehrke, R., & Kim, S. H. (2013). Impact of a teacher mentorship program on mentors' and mentees' perceptions of classroom practices and the mentoring experience. *Assessment for Effective Intervention, 38*(3), 154–162. https://doi.org/10.1177/1534508412457873

Morettini, B. (2016). Mentoring to support teacher retention in urban schools. *Teacher Education and Practice, 29*(2), 259–274.

Nguyen, T. D., Pham, L. D., Crouch, M., & Springer, M. G. (2020). The correlates of teacher turnover: An updated and expanded meta-analysis of the literature. *Educational Research Review, 31*, 1–17. https://doi.org/10.1016/j.edurev.2020.100355

Palmer, P. J. (1998). *The courage to teach: Exploring the inner landscape of a teacher's life*. Jossey-Bass.

Renbarger, R., & Davis, B. K. (2019). Mentors, self-efficacy, or professional development: Which mediate job satisfaction for new teachers? A regression examination. *Journal of Teacher Education and Educators, 8*(1), 21–34.

Ronfeldt, M., Loeb, S., & Wyckoff, J. (2013). How teacher turnover harms student achievement. *American Educational Research Journal, 50*(1), 4–36. https://doi.org/10.3102/0002831212463813

Sims, S., & Jerrim, J. (2020). *TALIS 2018: Teacher working conditions, turnover and attrition. statistical working paper.* Department for Education. https://assets.publishing.service.gov.uk/media/5f6484c28fa8f5107025c17a/TALIS_201_teacher_working_conditions_turnover_and_attrition.pdf

Sowell, M. (2017). Effective practices for mentoring beginning middle school teachers: Mentor's perspectives. *The Clearing House: A Journal of Educational Strategies, Issues and Ideas, 90*(4), 129–134. https://doi.org/10.1080/00098655.2017.1321905

Zee, M., & Koomen, H. M. Y. (2016). Teacher self-efficacy and its effects on classroom processes, student academic adjustment, and teacher well-being: A synthesis of 40 years of research. *Review of Educational Research, 86*(4), 981–1015. https://doi.org/10.3102/0034654315626801

Part 1

Wandering

1

Mutual Mentoring

Teacher-Friends

For this book, we outline what we mean by mentoring being mutually beneficial, how the relationship might focus on a topic or problem, and who might be the best choice as a teacher-friend for this adventure. Teaching provides many opportunities to work with a variety of professionals. Some teachers are our content area teammates, grade-level colleagues, and friends, and there is probably a nemesis in the mix. We learn new things from all these relationships, either covertly or overtly. We believe that we have mentors for many different teaching tasks and for many different seasons in our career.

According to Stake (2010), "Professional knowledge is the lore gained from working with others having similar training and depth of experience" (p. 13). If this is the case, teachers need feedback from their peers to deepen their professional knowledge—a way of understanding and valuing the lore. Peer coaching is one tool for facilitating teacher change, while acknowledging the logistical issues and necessary shifts in traditional teacher practice that coaching requires (Jewett & MacPhee, 2012). Peer feedback has the potential to contribute to teacher development, but it necessitates careful scaffolding to maximize impact. For our purposes, rather than coaching, we make an argument for mutual mentoring with teacher-friends.

Mutually Beneficial

Our mid-career mentoring approach is voluntary, non-punitive, and designed for positive outcomes. In the many ways mentoring can go right, it can also go wrong if the structure is constraining and expectations are not clearly articulated. For example, mentoring is not to be considered a therapy session. While personal and professional problems arise, a wise mentor guides where appropriate and suggests professional help where needed. Additionally, mentoring is not a one-way street. Mutually beneficial mentoring is a two-way relationship that emerges and develops over time. Better yet, mutual mentors choose each other outside of a typical professional development framework. We also believe that the best mentoring relationships are long term. They last beyond the initial adventure and grow in depth and breadth.

Mutual peer mentoring offers a uniquely reciprocal relationship that fosters both professional growth and emotional support. Unlike traditional hierarchical mentorship models, peer mentoring emphasizes equality and shared learning (Kroll et al., 2020; Swanson & Caskey, 2024). In peer mentoring, both participants contribute and benefit equally, allowing for an exchange of ideas, experiences, and feedback. Mutuality helps cultivate a sense of professional identity and belonging. This is important in teaching environments that can feel isolating. Teachers who share similar roles and responsibilities are better positioned to provide each other with advice and emotional validation.

One of the most significant benefits of peer mentoring is the transfer of tacit knowledge and referring to insights gained through personal experience that are not typically part of formal professional development (Swap et al., 2001). In education, this might include effective classroom management strategies, communication approaches with families, or culturally responsive teaching methods. Peer mentors serve as conduits for developing informal knowledge into explicit strategies that can be applied more broadly in classrooms and professional learning communities. This transfer supports continuous learning and improvement as well as complements formal training by addressing the practical, day-to-day challenges teachers face.

Furthermore, peer mentoring is associated with the development of critical skills such as ethical decision-making, problem-solving, and reflective thinking (Setó-Pamies & Papaoikonomou, 2016). These relationships often involve high levels of trust, empathy, and psychological safety, allowing teachers to discuss challenges openly and receive constructive, nonjudgmental feedback (Murrell et al., 2021). Teachers often look to their peers for guidance and inspiration. Colleagues who successfully handle professional challenges or take on leadership roles can motivate others to pursue similar goals (Kilduff, 1990; Zagenczyk et al., 2008). In this way, strong, reciprocal peer mentorship not only enhances individual skill development and emotional well-being but also helps shape the broader professional goals of teachers. Mentoring sharpens our skills through the use of critical and creative thinking and logical problem-solving.

Critical Thinking

It is important for teachers to be critical thinkers because their role goes far beyond delivering content; it involves making sound, purposeful judgments that directly impact student learning, classroom environments, and educational outcomes. According to Paul and Elder (2019), critical and creative thinking are interdependent. While creative thinking generates ideas and solutions, critical thinking evaluates their viability. In teaching, this means educators must both invent engaging lessons and assess whether those lessons meet learning objectives. A teacher cannot truly innovate in the classroom without simultaneously applying intellectual standards like clarity, accuracy, and relevance.

Critical thinking is a sign of personal maturity and depth of professional experience. To this end, we identify elements of critical thinking that signal when a teacher is highly astute and thus open to the challenge of mutual mentoring and an individualized professional development process. For example, teachers are constantly making decisions, from lesson planning to classroom management, and those decisions must be grounded in reasoned judgment, not habit or impulse. Similarly, teachers choose how to address issues by evaluating data, interpreting behavior, and making thoughtful, ethical decisions (Facione, 2015). Teachers always have a goal in mind. It may be whether that is improving student performance, fostering a safe learning environment, or adapting curriculum for diverse learners. Such goals require teachers to constantly monitor and assess whether their strategies are effective, using standards and criteria to guide improvement (Paul & Elder, 2019, p. 6). Without critical thinking, efforts become aimless, random, and ineffective.

Teaching is filled with complexities and unexpected challenges. Critical thinking equips teachers to reason through intricacies, pose meaningful problems, and design practical, thoughtful solutions. It supports informed decision-making in high-stakes contexts and encourages teachers to assess outcomes continually for improvement. Critical thinking is both an asset and a necessity for teachers. It enables them to thoughtfully maintain a clear, reflective, and goal-oriented approach to their work. As educators, critical thinking ensures that our teaching is not only informed but intentional and impactful. In terms of teacher-friend mentoring, only a critically thinking partner can provide a challenging and collaborative experience.

Teacher-friend mentoring is not for the faint of heart. A teacher's own critical thinking is essential for individual professional development; however, in contexts like mutual mentoring, it enables meaningful reflection, informed decision-making, and intentional collaboration. Critical thinking enhances the teacher-friend, mutual mentoring process in four ways:

- Critical thinking allows teachers to reflect deeply on their own beliefs, strategies, and experiences. As Mezirow (1990) and Taylor (1992) suggest, reflection helps teachers *identify what has worked in their practice, what hasn't, and how to grow*—before offering advice or guidance to others.
- Mentoring often involves helping peers navigate classroom challenges. Through critical thinking, a teacher can *analyze complex situations, weigh potential outcomes, and generate creative, yet viable, solutions.* As explained by Paul and Elder (2019), critical and creative thinking work together to both generate and evaluate options, a skill vital in mentoring others through their professional struggles.
- Critical thinking helps teachers *develop an understanding of their own thinking processes.* This self-awareness helps them approach mutual mentoring with humility and openness, recognizing that their own learning is ongoing.
- Mutual mentoring thrives on open, respectful dialogue. A critically thinking teacher is more likely *to ask meaningful questions, listen actively, and engage in dialogue that challenges both parties to grow.* This collaborative process is deeply rooted in purposeful, structured thinking.

In summary, a teacher's critical thinking is the foundation of an effective teacher-friend, mutual mentoring. It allows for self-reflection, reasoned support, and continuous improvement. By thinking critically, teachers can not only enhance their own development but also be more impactful, supportive of their peers. Choosing to be in a teacher-friend mentoring relationship is an example of one type of community of practice. A community of practice can be a tremendous asset to balance the passion and exhaustion of teaching.

Community of Practice

We like the idea of a community of practice because it is used in settings that require skills, choice, and growth. A community of practice is a group of people who share a common interest or concern and come together to fulfill their individual and collective goals (Wenger, 1998). In education, teachers choose to engage in many aspects of school. Typically, we belong to more than one community of practice. Teaching requires many professional partners and diverse communities, including professional learning groups in middle and high schools (content area planning), teams in middle school (English, social studies, math, and science teacher collaboration), and pairs or teams in elementary schools (grade-level collaboration). Teachers may join a certificate or degree program at the university, or they may be a coach. We connect the community of practice idea to our trekking metaphor because the community is teaching, while more specifically the *practice* can be each teacher-friend's skills and talents.

According to van Manen (2014), good talk "happens between two people who share an affinity or attachment to one another—not only to each other, but also to their shared world" (p. 36). Conversation is only part of the purpose, but it is also the collaboration that builds the ability to learn and grow from one another (van Manen, 2014). Mentoring between teacher-friends depends on good talk about their practice.

We acknowledge that beginning a mentoring relationship can be awkward. In a previous article on mentoring, we shared:

> *As with any new skill or relationship praxis starts slow, clumsily and requiring practice of multiple steps but over time repetition becomes muscle memory and habits of mind allowing for new challenges for the seasoned mentor and the maturing novice. Dialogue starts shallow and develops into deeper trusted conversation, ones that are risky, challenging assumptions.*
> (Swanson & Caskey, 2022, p. 15)

Dialogue and practice go hand in hand in learning how to hone the craft, learn the lore, and address job-embedded professional development in a casual and substantive way. Mentoring can have "professional benefits and positive impacts ... for the mentors and mentees" as well as "for schools, education systems and associated communities" (Hudson, 2013, p. 772). Throughout the mentoring interaction, mentors:

- introduce new knowledge and/or skills;
- use a repertoire of support tools to foster learning and bring about change in practice;
- help teachers connect theory and practice to their work; and
- acquire knowledge about how students learn and develop new pedagogical practice (Cordingley & Buckler, 2012).

These skills require dedicated professionals to have a growth mindset and an empathic approach. During a mentoring relationship, both teachers are comfortable having professional conversations that include "attentive listening, displaying a sense of humor, having empathy and asking questions…" (Hudson, 2016, p. 33). These contribute to building a mutually beneficial mentoring relationship.

Choosing a Teacher-Friend

A veteran teacher (5+ years) most likely does not want to be assigned a mentor, so then how do we go about choosing one that is or can be a teacher-friend. It goes without saying that a good friend may not make the best mentor, and likewise a randomly assigned teacher would not naturally fall into place as a friend.

First of all, teaching is an art. Artists learn skills not from reading about them in a book but through observing their peers. Tacit knowledge, knowledge that is not easily expressed, is what is shared through relationships. Mentoring is a means to improve practice in ways that are important to the mentee, such as behavior management, parent communications, and work-life balance. The experience and expertise that develops between 5 and 20 years in teaching is both practical and tacit.

It is important to find a teacher-friend who wants to share, wants to learn, and desires to build their practice. Mentoring discussions can go in multiple directions and have positive outcomes for participants. "Effective mentoring increases teacher retention … develops teaching expertise and confidence … reduces isolation … and fosters beginning teachers' reflection and development" (Smith, 2011, p. 316). A pair might choose to explore career advancement options such as a master's degree, an endorsement, or a certification program. For example, I (Karen) had two elementary teachers join the Ph.D. program. It was a great idea. These teachers supported each other through the ups and downs for three years, and they graduated together.

Our teacher-friend mentoring approach is different because it is designed specifically for mid-career teachers who choose to be in a mentoring relationship. It is designed to be intentional, acknowledging and blending teachers' professional life and personal life. Another difference is that you choose your teacher-friend, you are not assigned to a stranger. Choosing a partner is a mutual decision that recognizes the talents, humor, and special knowledge that each partner brings to the trek. We suggest that teacher-friend pairings be mid-career teachers, those who have been teaching for at least five years. By this point, teachers have evidence of effective teaching practices, contribute to school culture, and intentionally seek out professional development opportunities for themselves. Consider the following questions when you are selecting who you want to be in a teacher-friend mentoring relationship for the purpose of designing an individualized professional development plan.

- Who do you admire at your school?
- Who has a fresh approach to their career or teaching?
- Who talks about reading good books?
- Who belongs to an organization you're also interested in joining?
- Who laughs a lot?

- Who gives fresh insights in meetings?
- Who knows something you are interested in?
  - New technology
  - New children's books, Young Adult literature
  - Teaching adjunct classes at the college or university
- Who is doing a job you are interested in doing in the future?
  - Teacher on Special Assignment
  - Counselor
  - College-bound advisor
  - Principalship
  - Getting a degree (master's or doctoral)

The desired professional attributes in a mentoring partner also include a depth of understanding of the curriculum, instructional strategies, and assessment choices used in the district. The teacher-friend may be articulate about the school climate, school policies and procedures, and the diversity and equity of the students and community.

The personal qualities of your teacher-friend are also important. A teacher-friend is patient, open, and willing to build a trusting relationship, is organized, has a strong sense of efficacy, and is honest, positive, flexible, and collaborative. Teacher-friends are good listeners and able to hold multiple perspectives while learning and supporting a new teacher.

The role of the teacher-friend is to be a partner in *dialogue* and *practice* (Chapters 3 and 4). Therefore, choices and/or considerations include grade level, content area, proximity such as room placement, and schedule time to meet. The long-term goal is for the pair to use *dialogue* and *practice* to create their own reflective practice. Teacher-friends can also support one another through classroom observations, analyzing data collection, and reviewing professional goals and the steps to achieve those goals.

In a recent research summary, we discussed mentoring as career-long professional development. We asserted, "Mentoring can support developing pedagogies, curricula, culturally responsive teaching, and navigating the educational landscape. Mentoring can start at different stages to meet teachers' needs and to impact their efficacy" (Caskey & Swanson, 2023, p. 1). We also suggested that mentoring mid-career teachers stems from creating a community of practice rather than a one- or two-off professional development opportunity. We found mid-career teachers benefit from a mentoring space that creates opportunities to explore their teacher practice, to engage in intentional dialogue, and to embrace innovative, collaborative action. These experiences played a pivotal role in supporting mutually beneficial mentoring relationships in which teachers have empathy for one another and cheer each other on.

Teaching Phases

Teachers have taken a class(es) in child development or adolescent development learning that students change and grow in expected and unexpected ways and at different rates. However, adults grow and develop as well, which scholars termed adult development.

Regarding adult development, Berger (2012) used the term *constructive-development*, in which development focuses on meaning-making. *Constructive* is how each person creates meaning in their world by living it out. Whereas *development* is how each person makes meaning from the simple to the complex. Berger described that a constructive-developmental approach centers on "issues of authority, responsibility, ability to tolerate complexity and ambiguity" (p. 15). As adults develop, they are more able to consider the perspectives of others and take responsibility for their own emotions and choices. Berger explained that a person's perspective changes from black and white (right or wrong) to a more nuanced, graduated examination of the assumptions that define decision-making.

It is no surprise that a 22-year-old matures over their career, but a 50-year-old teacher can also continue to develop. As both walk through their career, they undergo change. According to Day and Gu (2014), teachers go through professional phases as they gain experience (see Table 1.1), which influences their identity and their professional development needs.

Understanding the phases of teaching and which phase you are in helps you to better understand yourself and your teaching peers. In the next section, we discuss teacher identity, which is specialized to the profession, and the skills teachers can employ to grow professionally.

Table 1.1 Phases of Teaching (Day & Gu, 2014)

Years of Teaching	Phase	Sub-Groups
0–3	Commitment: support and challenges	• Developing a sense of efficacy • Reduced sense of efficacy
4–7	Identity and efficacy in the classroom	• Sustaining a strong sense of identity, self-efficacy, and effectiveness • Identity, self-efficacy, and effectiveness are at risk
8–15	Managing changes in role and identity: growing tension and transition	• Sustaining engagement • Detachment and loss of motivation and commitment

Table 1.1 (Continued)

Years of Teaching	Phase	Sub-Groups
16–23	Work-life tensions: challenges to motivation and commitment	• Career advancement and good results have led to increased motivation and commitment • Sustaining motivation, commitment, and effectiveness • Workload, managing competing tensions, and career stagnation result in decreasing motivation, commitment, and effectiveness
24–30	Challenges to sustaining motivation	• Sustaining a strong sense of motivation • Holding on but losing motivation

Teacher Identity

A teaching identity is not a linear acquisition of skills and dispositions. A teacher's identity also encompasses the capacity for emotion, passion, and courage to teach (Palmer, 2017). It can also be useful to hold a complex perspective on a professional life. Complexity can provide a way of thinking about teaching that acknowledges the work of teaching. Research confirms the importance of teacher identity. In their review of literature, Hanna et al. (2019) found evidence:

> … that a strong and stable professional identity is positively related not only to emotional well-being, but also to the quality of teaching in the classroom. A well-developed professional identity can also improve teachers' confidence in their decision to work in education, and also their commitment to the profession.
>
> (p. 15)

Teacher identity has been studied for decades and continues to be difficult to define. Zembylas and Chubbuck (2018) evaluated previous research and summarized teaching identity as comprising the following four elements: emotion, narrative, discourse, and reflection. Who we are as teachers is built by our experiences, our goals, our schools, and our communities. We continually evolve as individuals and professionals as we learn and experience the world. Our "identities are a shifting amalgam of personal biography, culture, social influence, and institutional values which may change according to role or circumstance" (Day et al., 2006, p. 613). Therefore, it is important to hold tightly to our convictions about our students and classrooms but hold loosely to who we are and want to be in those spaces.

One of the frustrations with school or district-designed professional development is that it is a one-size-fits-all approach. Mid-career teachers need more autonomy to determine their own professional learning. As adult learners, teachers want to choose professional development that meets their immediate needs or long-term goals. In our mentoring approach, teachers get to choose their partner, meeting time, and purpose. This is referred to in the research literature as individualized professional development. We imagine a mentoring approach that is a yearlong or multi-year relationship that ebbs and flows with the school calendar, life events, and work demands.

We liken individualized professional development designed by two mid-career teachers to be similar to planning an adventure or a trek. In the following section, we introduce you to our trekking metaphor. We think this metaphor is fun, is useful, and provides clarity on mutual mentoring.

Teacher-Friend Trekking
Trekking, like teaching, can be a very solitary endeavor, yet teachers can also join other teachers along the way. These teacher-friend pairs can choose to trek together for a time to enrich their personal lives and build their professional practice. In doing so, they create their own community of practice.

In addition to the many parallel benefits between trekking and teacher-friend mentoring, we describe how this metaphor is woven through the book to illustrate these benefits for mid-career teacher-friends. Our metaphor hinges on the idea that trekking with teacher-friends can positively impact a teacher's identity related to family, work, love, education, hurt, recovery, and so on. In other words, engaging in back-and-forth dialogue, embracing innovative practices set in motion by challenging our assumptions, and exploring new possibilities.

Some define trekking as a long walk that lasts more than a few days, compared to hiking (Moira et al., 2021). In our metaphor, hiking might refer to short-term, isolated professional development offered by a school or district. When a person goes hiking, they intentionally return to their original starting point (usually where the car is parked). Trekking, on the other hand, is an activity designed by the teacher that targets specific personal and professional outcomes. It may last a semester, a year, or multiple years.

Trekking is defined as vigorous, long walks that do not necessarily follow a path. A clear destination is determined with a goal that takes multiple days to achieve. Another interesting element of trekking is that you do not return to the same place you began, whereas hikers always return to where they began. This allows for new discoveries and learning new terrain. Hiking can accommodate a variety of fitness levels, while trekking is more demanding and long-term.

Therefore, training for a trek is vital, and having experience is important. However, trekkers choose their destination, terrain, and time on the journey.

Much like trekking together, mentoring teacher-friends to work together happens over time and without rushing. They take a long view—looking at what lies ahead. They pace themselves because they know taking their time to think and draw upon their experience leads to better outcomes.

We introduced the trekking metaphor in the prologue. We have expanded the metaphor into a broad framework to help you identify each section or main idea throughout each chapter.

Boots

Boots represent our authentic self, our choices, and our comfort. There is evidence of our previous trips through the wear and tear on the boots. We intentionally identify broken-in boots because as mid-career teachers having a good pair of comfortable shoes has kept us going. Broken-in boots have molded to our foot shape. They do not give us blisters. They symbolize the strength and readiness required to face life's challenges and navigate difficult terrain.

We also put our emotions into this category. Teaching is an emotional job that requires caring deeply for students. We make both intellectually and emotionally informed decisions throughout the day and year.

Backpack

Backpacks hold what we choose to carry today. Tomorrow may be different. As goals are set, the possibility to reach a specific destination, are we really able to achieve that goal? Is a 10-mile trek reasonable for our fitness level and experience? The internal capacity to reach a goal is called agency. External structures are the things in place to support reaching the goal. For example, if I think we can do a 10-mile walk in one day (agency), the structures we put in place or use might include extra water and food, band-aids, knowledge of the terrain and weather prior to starting, extra layers of clothes, and so on.

We love to see what different people "carry around" with them in their backpack, purse, or teacher bag. Imagine if you dumped all the contents on the table and talked through why you carry those items around, how much would go in the garbage, how much is truly functional, and how much baggage you just do not know what else to do with now.

Before you begin trekking together and at key moments along the way, we offer *hydration stations*, *trail talks*, and *journal prompts*. These pause points may inspire you to reflect on what you choose to bring or carry every day or every school year. We invite you to examine your assumptions—both the ones that no longer serve a purpose and those that make the trek easier. We love our trekking metaphor because it beautifully captures and parallels a mid-career teaching mentoring approach.

Hydration Station

To sustain a long trek, we need to be diligent in drinking water often and refill our water bottles frequently. To this end, we provide sections in several chapters that summarize recent research on a topic. We strongly anchor this book in the literature and research intentionally to provide reliable information. We refer to these as hydration stations because it is important to be informed beyond our experience. Literature and research can challenge and expand our thinking and ability to solve problems.

Trail Talks

We provide a trail talk within most chapters. These conversations are meant to focus on a teacher-friend conversation about the topic of the chapter. These trail talks can take many forms:

- Walk and Talk (10 minutes, 20 minutes, or more). When we walk and talk versus sit and talk, the *quality of communication* feels different.
- Self-Talk on a Solo Walk (record ideas, questions, and responses on a phone while walking).

Keeping a Journal

Keeping a journal, journaling, is a great way to capture your thoughts and feelings. It allows you to capture your ideas in the moment and revisit them again in the future. The written format can "strengthen the reflective experience by creating artifacts of ideas of the mind" (Taylor, 2009, p. 9). Journaling supports cognitive and metacognition processes as you learn more about yourself as a teacher, your assumptions, and what you believe.

Table 1.2 Benefits of Trekking (Rideout, 2023)

Benefits of Trekking (Rideout, n.d.)	Benefits of Teacher-Friend Trekking
Enhances mental well-being and reduces stress from the hustle and bustle	
Fosters a sense of adventure and exploration	
Strengthens social bonds through shared experiences	
Provides opportunities for solitude and self-reflection	

In Table 1.2, we list the benefits of trekking. In the second column, we offer space for you and your partner to consider and record the possible benefits of teacher-friend trekking.

Reflection is both a critical and a creative process. As noted by Mezirow (1990) and Taylor (2009), reflection enables teachers to examine their beliefs and strategies, leading to deeper self-awareness and improved practices. This ongoing metacognitive process allows teachers to adapt, learn from experience, and remain effective in a changing educational landscape.

Conclusion

We contend that the pressures experienced in today's classrooms can quickly erase the positive aspects of teaching. According to Mosley et al. (2023), "Teacher stress continues to threaten the stability of the U.S. teaching workforce, but teacher mentoring, an increasingly prevalent type of teacher support, may uniquely support teachers with their risk-for-stress" (p. 20). Critical thinking helps teachers align their mentoring efforts with broader professional goals—both their own and their colleagues. It allows them to evaluate whether their mentoring strategies are effective, relevant, and aligned with school values or individual development plans.

We find the trekking metaphor for mentoring resonates with us because of the vast landscape our friendship has seen as we walk together. Our goal in introducing you to this approach to mentoring for long-term goals is to validate the important conversations that enhance our work. We agree that mentoring is "dynamic and synergistic, resulting in a mutually rewarding experience of personal development and learning" (Newsome, 2020, pp. 1166, 1168). As expressed by Berger and Johnston (2015), to thrive in a complex world, we all need to "be learning, every day and at every chance [we] get" (p. 65). We can approach work, home, and one another thinking, "What can I learn in this situation?"

In the next chapter, we discuss self-directed learning. We propose that you can take a solo trek or journey with a partner. The benefit of self-directed learning encompasses both professional development and mentoring with a teacher-friend. We describe how to choose a trekking partnership, whether long-term or short-term, designed to be mutually beneficial and without hierarchy. We include a self-study option so that transformative learning can occur for individual pacing.

References

Berger, J. G. (2012). *Changing on the job: Developing leaders for a complex world*. Stanford University Press.

Berger, J. G., & Johnston, K. (2015). *Simple habits for complex times: Powerful practices for leaders*. Stanford Business Books. https://doi.org/10.1515/9780804794251

Caskey, M., & Swanson, K. W. (2023). *Mentoring middle school teachers: Research summary*. https://www.amle.org/mentoring-middle-school-teachers-research-summary/

Cordingley, P., & Buckler, N. (2012). Mentoring and coaching for teachers' continuing professional development. In S. Fletcher, & C. Mullen (Eds.), *The SAGE handbook of mentoring and coaching in education* (pp. 215–227). SAGE Publications Ltd. https://doi.org/10.4135/9781446247549.n15

Day, C., & Gu, Q. (2014). Response to Margolis, Hodge and Alexandrou: Misrepresentations of teacher resilience and hope. *Journal of Education for Teaching: JET, 40*(4), 409–412. https://doi.org/10.1080/02607476.2014.948707

Day, C., Kington, A., Stobart, G., & Sammons, P. (2006). The personal and professional selves of teachers: Stable and unstable identities. *British Educational Research Journal, 32*(4), 601–616. https://doi.org/10.1080/01411920600775316

Facione, P. A. (2015). *Critical thinking: What it is and why it counts*. Measured Reasons.

Hanna, F., Oostdam, R., Severiens, S. E., & Zijlstra, B. J. H. (2019). Domains of teacher identity: A review of quantitative measurement instruments. *Educational Research Review, 27*, 15–27. https://doi.org/10.1016/j.edurev.2019.01.003

Hudson, P. (2013). Mentoring as professional development: 'Growth for both' mentor and mentee. *Professional Development in Education, 39*(5), 771–783. https://doi.org/10.1080/19415257.2012.749415

Hudson, P. (2016). Forming the mentor-mentee relationship. *Mentoring & Tutoring: Partnership in Learning, 24*(1), 30–43. https://doi.org/10.1080/13611267.2016.1163637

Jewett, P., & MacPhee, D. (2012). A dialogic conception of learning: collaborative peer coaching. *International Journal of Mentoring and Coaching in Education, 1*(1), 12–23. https://doi.org/10.1108/20466851211231594

Kilduff, M. (1990). The interpersonal structure of decision making: A social comparison approach to organizational choice. *Organizational Behavior and Human Decision Processes, 47*(2), 270–288. https://doi.org/10.1016/0749-5978(90)90039-c

Kroll, J., Blake-Beard, S., & McMillian-Roberts, K. (2020). An exploration of the peer group mentoring experiences of university female basketball athletes. *Mentoring & Tutoring: Partnership in Learning, 28*(2), 229–252. https://doi.org/10.1080/13611267.2020.1749355

Mezirow, J. (1990). *Fostering critical reflection in adulthood: A guide to transformative and emancipatory learning.* Jossey-Bass.

Moira, P., Mylonopoulos, D., & Terzoglou, E. (2021). Hiking tourism: Motives and behaviours: A case study. *TIMS. Acta, 15*(1), 13–22. https://doi.org/10.5937/timsact15-31825

Mosley, K. C., Playfair, E. C., Weppner, C. H., Balat, A., & Mccarthy, C. J. (2023). The bread and butter of a difficult profession: Mentoring as a resource for teacher stress. *Teachers and Teaching: Theory and Practice, 29*(1), 20–36. https://doi.org/10.1080/13540602.2022.2144819

Murrell, A. J., Blake-Beard, S., & Porter, D. M., Jr. (2021). The importance of peer mentoring, identity work and holding environments: A study of African American leadership development. *International Journal of Environmental Research in Public Health, 18*(9), 4920. https://doi.org/10.3390/ijerph18094920

Newsome, A. S. (2020). Pay it forward. *American Journal of Health-System Pharmacy, 77*(14), 1166–1168. https://doi.org/10.1093/ajhp/zxaa125

Palmer, P. J. (2017). *The courage to teach: Exploring the inner landscape of a teacher's life* (20th anniversary ed.). Wiley.

Paul, R., & Elder, L. (2019). *The nature and functions of critical & creative thinking.* Rowman & Littlefield.

Rideout, H. (2023). *Physical, mental and social benefits of hiking [Explained with studies].* https://myoutdoorbasecamp.com/benefits-of-hiking/

Setó-Pamies, D., & Papaoikonomou, E. (2016). A multi-level perspective for the integration of ethics, corporate social responsibility and sustainability (ECSRS) in management education. *Journal of Business Ethics, 136*(3), 523–538. https://doi.org/10.1007/s10551-014-2535-7

Smith, E. R. (2011). Faculty mentors in teacher induction: Developing a cross-institutional identity. *The Journal of Educational Research, 104*(5), 316–329. https://doi.org/10.1080/00220671.2010.482948

Stake, R. E. (2010). *Qualitative research: Studying how things work*. Guilford Press.

Swanson, K. W., & Caskey, M. M. (2022). Mentoring dialogue and practice: A transformative experience. *Journal of Transformative Learning, 9*(1), 8–17.

Swanson, K. W., & Caskey, M. M. (2024). Community of practice mentoring to retain middle school teachers. *Current Issues in Middle Level Education, 28*(1), Article 4. https://doi.org/10.20429/cimle.2024.280104

Swap, W., Leonard, D., Shields, M., & Abrams, L. (2001). Using mentoring and storytelling to transfer knowledge in the workplace. *Journal of Management Information Systems, 18*(1), 95–114. https://doi.org/10.1080/07421222.2001.11045668

Taylor, E. (2009). Fostering transformative learning. In J. Mezirow, E. W. Taylor, & Associates (Eds.), *Transformative learning in practice: Insights from community, workplace, and higher education* (pp. 3–17). Jossey-Bass.

Taylor, L. (1992). Mathematical attitude development from a Vygotskian perspective. *Mathematics Education Research Journal, 4*, 8–23. https://doi.org/10.1007/BF03217243

van Manen, M. (2014). *Phenomenology of practice. Meaning-giving methods in phenomenological research and writing*. Routledge.

Wenger, E. (1998). *Communities of practice: Learning, meaning and identity*. Cambridge University Press. https://doi.org/10.1017/cbo9780511803932

Zagenczyk, T. J., Gibney, R., Murrell, A. J., & Boss, S. R. (2008). Friends don't make friends good citizens, but advisors do. *Group & Organization Management, 33*(6), 760–780. https://doi.org/10.1177/1059601108326806

Zembylas, M., & Chubbuck, S. (2018). Conceptualizing 'teacher identity': A political approach. In P. Schutz, J. Hong, & F. D. Cross (Eds.), *Research on teacher identity: Mapping challenges and innovations* (pp. 183–193). Springer. https://doi.org/10.1007/978-3-319-93836-3_16

2

Self-Directed Learning

Trekking with a Partner or Solo

Mid-career teachers have a vast depth of knowledge developed through advanced degrees, years of professional development, lived experience, and being lifelong learners. In this chapter, we are going to make a case that teachers are the ideal candidates for self-directed learning professional development. We start by explaining the framework for self-directed learning and how it is a fresh approach when paired with teacher-friend mentoring. Self-directed learning honors curiosity and requires courage and integrity, as well as forges perseverance. We also acknowledge that teaching is a complex venture, and there is value in holding complexity when working through long-held beliefs and new ideas.

With complexity in mind, we approach self-directed learning through the examination of assumptions (Brookfield, 2009). We can intentionally examine our assumptions and challenge existing ideas in four categorical ways:

- Interaction and conversation with peers
- Reading and implementing a new theory
- Asking students about their experiences
- Having honest conversations about our prior experiences that formed the decisions we currently make regarding personal and professional life

Next, we discuss how and where to find like-minded teacher-friends such as book clubs and professional organizations. We spend some time looking at unexpected friends through reverse mentoring, where new teachers have skills that could benefit them professionally. We want to acknowledge their skills and make sure that we do not discount them based on being a novice.

Ultimately, we encourage you to choose a partner that might be faster than you, older than you, younger than you, or more skilled in a specific area. If you are on a solo journey, how do you use self-directed learning to inform your practice, stay on track, and meet your goals? Whether you are trekking alone or trekking with a teacher-friend, the outcome can be productive, engaging, beautiful, and transformative.

Self-Directed Learning

One of the many ways trekking with teacher-friends is different from traditional mentoring is the focus on the concept of self-directed learning (Knowles, 1975). Knowles (1975) posited that adults have a learning framework that is different from younger students. Robinson and Persky (2020) restated this notion that self-directed learning is defined as creating experiences that empower learners to make decisions about what they want to become proficient in knowing. This is a definition that resonates with us when we are talking about teachers. Holland (1972) added to Knowles' ideas in that the vocational code he developed categorizes teachers as social, artistic, and enterprising. Social, artistic, and enterprising describe most teachers we know. In fact, we work best with the freedom to be artistic; socialize with students, parents, and other teachers; and employ our enterprising spirit through creating new ways to think about and approach curriculum and pedagogy.

We offer this background because teachers are a creative bunch. We agree with Lemmetty and Collin (2021), who found three elements of self-directed learning relating to adult learning:

- A combination of individual and collective action
- Solving common problems through dialogue and discussions
- The organizational culture framing self-directed learning in creative activity

In other words, self-directed learning mentoring can be a linear (novice to expert) process or a cyclical process that repeats as we grow individually or in the company of other teacher-friends. A self-directed learning cycle simplifies and identifies these processes:

- Identify a learning gap or issue
- Approach closing the gap through resources

- Reflect on the process and what it elicits
- Apply the new knowledge to the situation, whether personal or professional (Brockett & Hiemstra, 2018).

Self-directed learning is about embracing lifelong, self-identified learning, whether in our personal or professional lives. The goal is to advance from a novice thinker to an expert thinker—to become a critical thinker. What is ideal about self-directed learning is evolutionary in the development of skills and attitudes. What is ideal about self-directed learning for the teacher-friend model of professional development is that personal attributes play a significant role; they matter. Learning does not separate personal and professional growth; instead, it bridges and blends them. We think four attributes among many can particularly enhance the teacher-friend and solo-trekking sense of growth: *curiosity, flexibility, integrity, and perseverance*. Lastly, we discuss complexity, which acknowledges that at the core of teaching the work and aspirations are not simple but rather intricate and multifaceted.

Curiosity

What does it mean to be professionally curious? Most veteran teachers might say that schoolwide professional learning can be formulaic and a one-size-fits-all approach can kill curiosity. We suggest that a teacher-friend mentoring approach can provide a rich environment in which curiosity can thrive. According to Ricotta et al. (2022), curiosity "is dynamic and influenced by multiple factors, including a learner's mindset and intellectual humility—one must be able to say, 'I don't know' and identify learning gaps" (p. 533). Those gaps can develop into an ideal trekking adventure for a teacher-friend pair to explore.

Flexibility

The concept of flexibility is a multifaceted idea when applied to mentoring, professional growth, and self-directed learning. Flexibility refers to the ability to bend without breaking. Teaching is a daily exercise in flexibility. We adjust to student needs, alternative schedules, differentiated student ability, and administrative demands. In a similar fashion, cognitive flexibility refers to an individual's ability to assess a situation, adjust their behavior, and adjust to their changing environment.

The teacher-friend and solo-trekking model can provide support to increase our flexibility in many ways. Mentoring provides a sounding board for partners to experiment with and discuss new ideas. These conversations can increase a teacher's openness to new ideas, executive functioning, manage an emotional response to stress, and the ability to respond well to unexpected changes. Finally, self-directed learning can be "described as a learner who has the ability to adapt creatively in response to new challenges, a flexible learner embraces new ideas, and appreciates new perspectives" (Ricotta et al., 2022, p. 533). Flexibility is not only learning something new but having the higher order ability to transfer it to a teaching situation.

Integrity
In any profession and in any relationship, integrity is key to being successful. Integrity refers to a person's character to choose honesty, hold to moral and ethical principles. Interestingly, integrity also means to be whole. We appreciate how both definitions provide insight into integrity for teacher-friends and solo-trekking. In the context of self-directed learning, integrity refers to "accountability and responsibility not only to oneself (internal motivator), but also to [students, teachers and parents]" (Ricotta et al., 2022, p. 533). This includes being self-aware and understanding your own decisions, metacognition, to consider why you think the way you do.

Perseverance
"You can do hard things" is a phrase we use with our students frequently. The goal is to encourage them to keep working until they have achieved the desired outcome. This is perseverance, a desirable skill in both kids and adults. It is during stressful times that attributes such as resilience and perseverance can be built. For example, teacher-friends may discuss one student all year long and feel like they are not making any progress. However, self-directed learning could prompt the pair to read, question their existing assumptions, and apply possible solutions. Perseverance means to stay open, engaged, rather than repeating a tired pattern.

Complexity in Practice
We have discussed issues related to teacher retention, and we found no simple answers. What we know for sure is that the problems and solutions are complex. It is in our nature to simplify difficult situations, to choose a quick solution. However, as we mature as teachers, we learn that if we can resist simplification in exchange for holding onto the complexity of a problem, the possibilities and depth of a solution can be rich. So, what does that mean? According to Berger and Johnston (2015):

> *Complexity is about getting our heads around what is possible (because anything can happen) rather than what is probably going to happen (which is determined from what has happened before). This shift—from trying to get your head around what is most likely to happen to trying*

to get your head around what is in the field of possibilities—is much bigger than it sounds ... Our general pattern is to prune and simplify.

(p. 11)

Complexity seems like the best place to start in planning what a trekking journey will entail. This is not a trip to the grocery store. It is choosing to take a trip to somewhere new and a choice not to return to the mindset of simply thinking about a topic or challenge that we started with in the beginning. As suggested by Berger and Johnston (2015):

... if we are going to create new patterns of behavior for thinking and acting in this new world. We need to talk to one another differently, gather information differently, build strategies and plan for the future in new ways. We need new habits of mind that stretch and expand us to deal in more thoughtful ways with the complexity the world offers.

(p. 12)

They also suggest that a complex system of problem-solving includes "conversation, discovery, and experimentation" (p. 53). We argue that conversations are most effective when we choose a trusted teacher-friend. However, if a teacher-friend is not already part of your professional circle, how do you find one? The next section provides some ideas.

Teacher-Friends

Choosing a mentoring or trekking partner is essential to meet your goals. We highlight a few options to find a partner. The first is having common interests within the larger professional development goal, such as content area, grade level, or educational goal. With common interests in mind, we provide a short list of how and where you might find a like-minded partner.

Common Interests

Common interest is a natural place to begin finding a teacher-friend. Teams and content area professional learning groups are a logical place to find like-minded colleagues. Support teachers such as special education, counselors, ELL (English Language Learner), or MTSS (Multi-Tiered Support System) coordinators are also possible candidates to be a teacher-friend. The goal is to choose a partner who will elicit and participate in fresh insights and new conversations. One suggestion is to find a like-minded trekker to determine what you are interested in learning more about. We have listed places to consider finding a teacher-friend with common interests but a new partnership.

We met through the Association for Middle Level Education several years ago. We both had a commitment to middle-level education and were both previously middle-level teachers, and, when we met, we were both professors working with teachers and doctoral students at the university. This relationship was a good fit for us both professionally. Personally, it turns out we both had only child—a daughter and wonderful spouses. These commonalities gave us many pathways to be vulnerable, ask questions, give advice, and hold one another accountable.

It is worth considering that your trekking partner is not in the classroom next door, but across the country. The joy of living in the 21st century is that we can talk daily, weekly, or monthly face-to-face from our living rooms. For example, Micki lives in Portland, Oregon, and Karen lives in Colorado Springs, Colorado. We meet twice a week to talk, share, write together, dream, and talk about our families.

Organizations

Educational organizations are a great way to meet teachers with common interests. A Google search of "educational organizations" provides a vast list of non-profit groups that are worth considering. There are groups for elementary, middle, and secondary levels. There is a group for every content and exploratory subject, from STEM (science, technology, engineering, math) to foreign language.

You might choose to join an organization at the state, national, or international level. You might choose to read their publications or contribute your ideas and writing for publication. Organizations provide specialized professional development through in-person and virtual means. Many educational organizations also have yearly conferences around the country.

Book Studies or Club

If you are looking for a short-term opportunity to meet teachers with common interests, you may wish to attend a book study either at your school or district level or online. For example, Scholastic has several book clubs for teachers to join. If you have read a book and want to do a book study, consider contacting your professional development office and offering to lead the book study. Teachers can receive professional development credits for this, and you might even get paid for your time.

Writing Groups

In a similar path (to keep with the metaphor), writing groups are also an option for finding teachers with similar gifts, goals, and hobbies. A writing group could be one that is for fun, if you are working on the next great novel or if you want to publish your first article. Again, a Google search provides a plethora of online options in which joining the group provides time, structure, and at times feedback to support a project moving forward.

These are only three of the many places to meet that new teacher-friend. Another strategy to consider is to look beyond your age group or teachers with similar years of experience. Next, we expand on the idea of partnering intentionally with a new teacher. This is not to be their mentor but to trek together and learn from one another. You may become unexpected teacher-friends.

Reverse Mentoring

Reverse mentoring taps into the skills of the new teacher. Understanding how we are similar and different from our colleagues is important. The research is abundant on reverse mentoring. Teachers who are new to the profession come out of college with fresh pedagogy and often with preparation that is vastly different from veteran teachers.

Mid-career teachers already possess a well-developed set of teaching skills. However, considering the quickly changing nature of education, we know how valuable it is to tap into the skills that newly minted teachers bring to the classroom. Reverse mentoring is an intergenerational mentoring relationship where the more experienced person is the mentee, and the younger person is the mentor. It is based on the concept that younger mentors have fresh and new ideas and skills to share (Chaudhuri & Ghosh, 2012). Reverse mentoring extends the traditional model of the older, more experienced teacher mentoring the new teacher. Early career teachers can share innovative pedagogy or technology skills that benefit the more experienced teacher. Reverse mentoring not only honors new teacher voices, but it also eases them into a community of practice.

Hydration Station: Benefits of Reverse Mentoring

We wondered about its effectiveness and the benefits of reverse mentoring for teachers. For this reason, we reviewed several research articles to satisfy our curiosity. Researchers offered the following findings about reverse mentoring.

- ◆ Reverse mentoring benefits the mentees, mentors, and organizations. The exchange of information and skills supports "employees socialize, providing support and direction in career planning, and increasing job satisfaction, organizational commitment, and engagement" (Chaudhuri et al., 2022, p. 14).
- ◆ The senior mentee can add a few more skills to their repertoire, and the junior mentor can benefit too through gaining information

access, appreciation, professional respect, and personal fulfillment and satisfaction (Harvey et al., 2009).
- Among the benefits gained by implementing reverse mentoring are increased motivation, engagement, retention, performance and productivity, and generational equity (Garg et al., 2021).
- "Informal reverse mentoring can be defined as an on-the-job spontaneous relational exchange of knowledge, feedback, and ideas where senior employees benefit through gaining a new perspective or skill and the junior employees gain self-esteem and respect through contributing to their senior colleagues' professional development" (Chaudhuri et al., 2022, p. 15).
- In the process, reverse mentoring enhances intergenerational competencies, challenging the hierarchical structure and strengthening the leadership pipeline (Garg et al., 2021).

We think these are an encouraging set of findings. There are many benefits to partnering with a new teacher when being a teacher-friend is at the heart of the relationship, rather than being their traditional mentor.

We designed the next section for starting a conversation with your teacher-friend to choose a topic which will eventually be your trekking adventure. However, all relationships require good communication to set goals and share ideas. Teaching is a time-intensive profession; therefore, to be successful teacher-friends it is important to acknowledge individual time constraints and priorities. The best model is for a teacher-friend relationship to be mutually beneficial.

Communication, Goals, and Expectations

A trek can be short, such as three miles in one morning, or it can be 30 miles and take three days. You might trek for fun, for sanity, or for a cause. Trekking for you might be meditative and quiet or a loud adventure with friends. However, if you are trekking with one or more teacher-friends, it is important to set some boundaries so that everyone feels safe, heard, and seen. Teacher-friend mentoring is a reciprocal partnership in which both trekking partners contribute and thus experience positive rewards from their interactions. Such partnerships are ideal for mid-career teachers.

We argue that two-way and mutually beneficial mentoring relationships create the conditions for teacher-friends to grow and thrive professionally and personally. Such mentoring relationships are "dynamic and synergistic, resulting in a mutually rewarding experience of personal development and learning" (Newsome, 2020, pp. 1166, 1168). This style of relationship allows experienced teachers to pursue their own interests and determine their own path. Components of mutually beneficial relationships include:

- actively learning and growing with each other (Ragins, 2016);
- trusting and respecting one another as well as the mentoring processes and practices (Hudson, 2016; Sowell, 2017);
- developing a supportive and collaborative relationship (Weimer, 2019);
- building an equal and empowering partnership (Weimer, 2019); and
- engaging in purposeful work about their teaching practice (Swanson & Caskey, 2024).

Yes, active participation is an integral and mutually part of relationships (Blake-Beard, n.d.). Teacher-friends work closely together and contribute to an ongoing dialogue about their teaching practice. Because teachers have a range of teaching and generational experiences, they can hold unique perspectives about teaching and learning. So, as trekking partners must feel safe and empowered to pose questions, offer suggestions, discuss challenges, disclose uncertainties, reveal biases, and celebrate successes. Using "open communication within a supportive, friendly and personally nonjudgmental environment," they can traverse unfamiliar ground (Hudson, 2016, p. 39).

Trekking with a partner also fosters a sense of belonging. As teacher-friends, you form your own community of practice (Wenger, 1998), which can reduce feelings of professional isolation (Holland, 2018) and improve your well-being (Cherkowski & Walker, 2019). In fact, belonging is at the heart of mentoring. It is important to determine common goals that include a purpose and a timeframe. These keep the trek on track by keeping teacher-friends headed in the same direction and to the same destination.

We intend trekking to be accessible for teacher-friends but also for those who want to study alone. In literature, scholars refer to this solo work as self-study.

Self-Mentoring or Self-Study

In the teaching profession, one form of reflective practice is action or teacher research. It is a familiar process in which teachers choose a topic that they want to learn about, implement, and improve upon and use an action research framework to organize their work. In action research, teachers start with a question, research new ideas, implement those ideas, gather either anecdotal or student data, review the findings, and then ask a new question. Self-mentoring is a similar process with complementary components. During the exploratory process, the teacher collects data (qualitative and quantitative), takes notes, and is reflective about the process and what they are learning. The process of intentionally examining our personal behaviors, considering what the rewards are for learning and implementing new ways and ideas, and improving our thinking about teaching and life are the key to successful self-mentoring (Carr et al., 2017).

Self-mentoring is effective for all stages of a teaching career. "Self-mentoring requires an individual to assemble a realistic, accurate assessment of him/herself with the goal of crafting an 'ideal self' to heighten job performance, career progression, or personal ambitions" (Carr et al., 2015). There are four development levels:

- Self-awareness (what do I lack or want)
- Self-development (what resources are available to strengthen my understanding)
- Self-reflection (when I think about my progress or application to practice—what have I learned)
- Self-monitoring (what is my next step or how am I continuously or effectively implementing what I've learned) (Carr et al., 2017)

As specified in the name, self-mentoring is a solo trek. You are your coach and your own mentor. You set your goals and determine the means to reach those goals. However, much like solo-trekking you will meet people and have meaningful conversations along the way. Stephen Brookfield (2009) wrote about self-directed learning and identified four elements that can influence and speak into our learning as teachers:

1. Theory—the reading and implementation of research and literature to improve practice and challenge existing assumptions
2. Students—asking students how they are experiencing your class, lessons, rules, expectations, and so on
3. Peers—leveraging skilled colleagues to inform your thinking about curriculum, instruction, school culture, and life
4. Our autobiography—knowing yourself and how your story positively or negatively informs your personal and professional decisions and reactions

When undertaking self-directed learning, it is important to seek out multiple perspectives on the work, collaboration, and next steps. It is equally important to choose individuals whom you trust will give you honest and productive feedback. We share more about Brookfield's (2009) four lenses and their impact on teacher practice in Chapter 6.

As mentioned previously regarding action research, self-mentoring involves planning around a question or idea. Self-mentoring requires a commitment of time and self-motivation to be successful in maximizing the time spent on strengthening new skills.

Teaching is not the only profession that embraces self-mentoring. Self-mentoring is also evident in nursing (Gordon & Melrose, 2011). According to Gordon and Melrose (2011), nurses can use self-mentoring to gain professional knowledge and implement that knowledge into practice. Take a few moments to scan our summary table of Gordon and Melrose's five practical strategies, along with possible activities to improve nurses' experiences (see Table 2.1).

Table 2.1 Self-Mentoring Strategies and Possible Activities (Gordon & Melrose, 2011)

Strategy	Activities
Reflection	• Thinking about past events and circumstances, about role models, and work • These reflections can help reclaim the courage and spirit to make a difference
Continuous learning	• Subscribe to a journal • Attend an in-person or virtual conference • Search for evidence-based research on the topic • Join an organization to build a network of information and support • Choose to supervise a student teacher
Making a plan	• Assess your learning needs • Identify your educational philosophy • Create a plan to meet your educational or personal goal • Organize the steps and process • Implement the process • Evaluate the plan and your progression
Volunteering	• Present what you have learned to others • Support and mentor new teachers
Communicating	• Share your story and journey • Share the importance of designing a journey • Share resources • Share the best habits of mind that made self-mentoring as professional development useful, such as openness to new ideas, willingness to submit one's ideas and beliefs to critical reflection, and confidence in the power of collaborative learning

After scanning Gordon and Melrose's (2011) five practical strategies and the related activities, consider the implications for the teaching profession and particularly your practice. What are the similarities and differences?

We believe that self-mentoring is an effective way to evaluate, challenge, and educate ourselves when traditional mentoring is either not available or not desired. The elements of self-mentoring provide a framework that is much like a map used in a solo trek. The teacher has several choices and decisions that impact the destination, speed, and success of the trip. It is important to consider that self-mentoring may work in the long-term or short-term because it can help you solve specific problems.

Gear to Support Self-Directed Learning

Now it is time to look at tools that can support self-directed learning—ones you can use when trekking solo or with another person. As teachers, you likely already use the two tools we recommend: a camera and a journal. You may use these to capture a moment and preserve it for future reference.

Camera

Reflection can also be a single moment or situation that is captured like a photograph. A picture allows us to revisit a situation, notice the details, and fill in the blanks about what happened before and after the event. We believe a camera is an invaluable metaphor for teaching and learning. You probably do as well. We know that others, such as Dorothea Lange, agree.

What makes a camera so useful for self-directed learning? A camera helps you focus your observations and capture specific places, events, or moments. You can use a camera to look ahead, to snap photos along the way, and view them again following a trek. When you hold the camera, you get to choose where to point the lens, how to frame the experience, and what to preserve.

As mid-career teachers, you are adept at seeing your students as they grow and learn. You likely also notice your colleagues as they grow professionally.

- But what about yourself?
- We invite you to pause and take a selfie. What do you see?
  - Are you fully present in the moment you took the selfie?
  - Can you see curiosity reflected or an eagerness to learn in your eyes? If not, what do you want to see in your selfie?
- We encourage you to point the camera at your teaching practice.
  - What do you notice?

- What is pleasing or satisfying in your practice?
- What is missing?

Answering these questions may help you to identify and focus on a specific pathway for self-directed learning on your trekking adventure.

Journals

Journals represent teacher reflection. Journals and cameras represent the teacher's reflection. Conflict or wonder tends to spark reflection. Reflection fills the spaces between the past and the future. Reflection can be a process that we capture in our journals as we look for reasons, patterns, or answers.

Why keep a journal? Keeping a journal is an ideal way for capturing your ideas or exploring new ideas alongside a teacher-friend. Journaling can feel strange or like a burden. Yet, it can be a positive habit. For instance, journaling may relieve stress because once you write about an issue or something on your mind, you may be able to stop ruminating or thinking about it. Journaling can also bring you feelings of accomplishment when you see progress on your goals over time.

Some refer to this as a learning or reflective journal (Shepherd, 2006). In addition, you can use your journal as we do for holding space for creative ideas, resources, and to-do lists.

What kind of journal works well for trekking? We suggest keeping a bound journal to keep your ideas in one place. A bound journal can help you refrain from tearing out and discarding pages, which may happen when carrying a spiral-bound journal. We believe all your ideas—even those you abandon along the trek—are worth keeping.

Perhaps you already keep a journal and know how to use it. If you are not currently keeping a journal, we hope you will accept our invitation to experiment with journaling. You can pick a journal that appeals to you. Some teachers like a compact journal, while others prefer a letter-size journal. The good news is that both can easily slip inside your professional backpack. You can use your journal for planning a trek, taking notes along the trail, and reflecting on your experiences after the trek. Much like the camera metaphor, a journal can be a useful tool for self-directed learning. You can literally use it to help you plan, focus, and reflect on your professional experiences.

Once you have a journal, we suggest you try freewriting. Freewriting is a creative and practical way to generate ideas, clarify meaning, and tap your own voice (Elbow, 1998). We believe this type of writing not only captures your thoughts, but it may also set your creative side "free." A related journal-keeping activity is focused on freewriting (Stevens & Caskey, 2016).

With focused freewriting, you focus on a predetermined and specific topic. We know it is another powerful way to explore your own thinking.

We offer some examples of trekking prompts for a focused freewrite that may be meaningful for teacher-friend journaling:

- Write about a time when you overcame an obstacle on the trail or at school.
- Reflect on your favorite hiking trail or learning experience and why it holds a special place in your heart.
- Write about a time when you hiked in a new place and how it made you feel.
- Reflect on the people you met on the trail or throughout your career and how they impacted your experience.
- Write a letter to someone you wish could trek with you and tell them why.
- Reflect on how hiking or teaching has changed you as a person.
- Write about the different emotions such as success and exhaustion, which you felt on your hike or teaching, and why.

We encourage you to begin or continue journaling about your teaching practice and trekking adventures. Whether you take a solo trek or trek with a teacher-friend, we believe journaling can be a useful and purposeful strategy for you.

Journal Prompt: Focused Freewriting

Use these steps to guide a focused free write in your journal.

- Open your journal.
- Select a topic.
- Write the topic in your journal.
- Set a timer for 10 minutes.
- Write about your topic for 10 minutes.
- If needed, use these guiding questions:
  - What is the topic?
  - What interests me about this topic?
  - Why do I care about this topic?
  - What do I already know about this topic?
  - What do I want to know?
  - Who else might be interested in this topic?
- When the timer sounds, stop writing.

- Read and reflect on what you have written.
- Write one to two sentences about your insights about what you have written.

(Adapted from Stevens & Caskey, 2016)

Conclusion

The ultimate decision about whether to trek solo or with teacher-friends is deeply personal and quite practical. Teacher-friends are helpful for accruing new perspectives and gaining valuable insights through mutual or reverse mentoring. We view self-directed learning as both a personal and professional disposition to better our understanding of ourselves and our teaching.

As mid-career teachers, you have a wealth of expertise and a great deal of experience. Both of these will serve you well as you engage in self-directed learning. You get to choose your own trekking adventure. Remember that, when you are trekking, you do not return to the place where you started; rather, you go to new places. You open yourself to growing professionally and personally.

We encourage you to design your own adventure as you explore this book. You may choose to read what is most relevant or immediate to your life, peruse parts of chapters, or sample the activities. It is up to you. If you a planning to take a long trek, you may find value in reading the chapters in order and engaging with the activities. It is completely up to you! Whatever path you decide to take, we want you to enjoy the adventure.

References

Berger, J. G., & Johnston, K. (2015). *Simple habits for complex times: Powerful practices for leaders*. Stanford Business Books.

Blake-Beard, S. (n.d.). *Mentoring: Creating mutually empowering relationships*. https://womensleadership.stanford.edu/resources/voice-influence/mentoring-creating-mutually-empowering-relationships

Brockett, R. G., & Hiemstra, R. (2018). *Self-direction in adult learning: Perspectives on theory, research and practice* (eBook). Routledge.

Brookfield, S. D. (2009). Self-directed learning. In R. Maclean, & D. Wilson (Eds.), *International handbook of education for the changing world of work: Bridging academic and vocational learning* (pp. 2615–2627). Springer.

Carr, M. L., Holmes, W., & Flynn, K. (2017). Using mentoring, coaching, and self-mentoring to support public school educators. *The Clearing House: A*

Journal of Educational Strategies, Issues and Ideas, 90(4), 116–124. https://doi.org/10.1080/00098655.2017.1316624

Carr, M. L., Pastor, D. K., & Levesque, P. J. (2015). Learning to lead: Higher education faculty explore self-mentoring. *International Journal of Evidenced Based Coaching and Mentoring, 13*(2), 1–13.

Chaudhuri, S., & Ghosh, R. (2012). Reverse mentoring: A social exchange tool for keeping the Boomers engaged and Millennials committed. *Human Resource Development Review, 11*(1), 55–76. https://doi.org/10.1177/1534484311417562

Chaudhuri, S., Ghosh, R., & Park, S. (2022). The missing voices of learning and development professionals: Factors influencing formal and informal practices of reverse mentoring. *New Horizons in Adult Education & Human Resource Development, 34*(4), 14–30. https://doi.org/10.1002/nha3.20367

Cherkowski, S., & Walker, K. (2019). Mentorship for flourishing in schools: An explicit shift toward appreciative action. *International Journal of Mentoring and Coaching in Education, 8*(4), 345–360. https://doi.org/10.1108/IJMCE-02-2019-0018

Elbow, P. (1998). *Writing without teachers* (2nd ed.). Oxford University Press. https://doi.org/10.1093/oso/9780195120165.001.0001

Garg, N., Murphy, W., & Singh, P. (2021). Reverse mentoring, job crafting and work-outcomes: The mediating role of work engagement. *Career Development International, 26*(2), 290–308. https://doi.org/10.1108/CDI-09-2020-0233

Gordon, K. P., & Melrose, S. (2011). Self-mentoring: 5 practical strategies to improve retention of long-term care nurses. *Canadian Nursing Home, 22*(2), 14–19.

Harvey, M., McIntyre, N., Thompson Heames, J., & Moeller, M. (2009). Mentoring global female managers in the global marketplace: Traditional, reverse, and reciprocal mentoring. *The International Journal of Human Resource Management, 20*(6), 1344–1361. https://doi.org/10.1080/09585190902909863

Holland, E. (2018). Mentoring communities of practice: What's in it for the mentor? *International Journal of Mentoring and Coaching in Education, 7*(2), 110–126. https://doi.org/10.1108/IJMCE-04-2017-0034

Holland, J. L. (1972). The present status of a theory of vocational choice. In J. M. Whiteley, & A. Resnikoff (Eds.), *Perspectives on vocational development* (pp. 35–59). American Personnel and Guidance Association.

Hudson, P. (2016). Forming the mentor-mentee relationship. *Mentoring & Tutoring: Partnership in Learning, 24*(1), 30–43. https://doi.org/10.1080/13611267.2016.1163637

Knowles, M. S. (1975). *Self-directed learning: A guide for learners and teachers*. The Adult Education Company.

Lemmetty, S., & Collin, K. (2021). Self-directed learning in creative activity: An ethnographic study in technology-based work. *The Journal of Creative Behavior, 55*(1), 105–119. https://doi.org/10.1002/jocb.438

Newsome, A. S. (2020). Pay it forward. *American Journal of Health-System Pharmacy, 77*(14), 1166–1168. https://doi.org/10.1093/ajhp/zxaa125

Ragins, B. R. (2016). From the ordinary to the extraordinary: High-quality mentoring relationships at work. *Organizational Dynamics, 45*(3), 228–244. https://doi.org/10.1016/j.orgdyn.2016.07.008

Ricotta, D. N., Richards, J. B., Atkins, K. M., Hayes, M. M., McOwen, K., Soffler, M. I., Tibbles, C. D., Whelan, A. J., & Schwartzstein, R. M. (on behalf of Millennium Conference 2019 writing group). (2022). Self-directed learning in medical education: Training for a lifetime of discovery. *Teaching and Learning in Medicine, 34*(5), 530–540. https://doi.org/10.1080/10401334.2021.1938074

Robinson, J. D., & Persky, A. M. (2020). Developing self-directed learners. *American Journal of Pharmaceutical Education, 84*(3), 847512. https://doi.org/10.5688/ajpe847512

Shepherd, M. (2006). Using a learning journal to improve professional practice: A journey of personal and professional self-discovery. *Reflective Practice, 7*(3), 333–348. https://doi.org/10.1080/14623940600837517

Sowell, M. (2017). Effective practices for mentoring beginning middle school teachers: Mentor's perspectives. *The Clearing House: A Journal of Educational Strategies, Issues and Ideas, 90*(4), 129–134. https://doi.org/10.1080/00098655.2017.1321905

Stevens, D. D., & Caskey, M. M. (2016, October). *Bridge over the choppy waters of academic writing: Strategies to support EdD students across their program*. Carnegie Project for the Educational Doctorate, Augusta, GA.

Swanson, K. W., & Caskey, M. M. (2024). Community of practice mentoring to retain middle school teachers. *Current Issues in Middle Level Education, 28*(1), 1–12. https://doi.org/10.20429/cimle.2024.280104

Weimer, K. R. (2019). Maximizing mentoring relationships. *General Music Today, 32*(2), 12–17. https://doi.org/10.1177/1048371318805226

Wenger, E. (1998). *Communities of practice: Learning, meaning and identity*. Cambridge University Press. https://doi.org/10.1017/cbo9780511803932

3

Communication

Dialogue, Conversation, and Good Talk

Communication is integral to the teaching profession. Throughout the school year, teachers communicate with their students, parents, and colleagues. As you know, these exchanges can boost understanding and foster positive relationships. We suggest that communicating while on a trekking adventure is not only pleasurable but also fundamental for thriving along the journey. Think about it, the pleasure you feel when exchanging stories of past adventures, sharing impressions of the natural world as it unfolds in front of you, or anticipating what you will discover together along your journey.

According to Nhất Hạnh (2013), "We communicate to be understood and to understand others" (p. 41). He explains that we are continually communicating with ourselves, with other people, and with the world around us. We communicate through our thoughts, words, and actions. We embrace Nhất Hạnh's thinking about communication as it relates to mutual mentoring between teacher-friends or self-mentoring.

Communication between teacher-friends is essential for finding new ground together. Teacher-friends rely on various types of communication, including dialogue, conversation, and good talk (see Figure 3.1). We view dialogue as more intentional, intellectual, and inclusive communication; conversation as less formal yet vital social communication; and good talk as a more intimate type of communication, the heart work. In this chapter, we explore these types of communication that you and your teacher-friend can use on your trekking adventures.

We begin with and emphasize dialogue. Because of its intentional nature, we believe dialogue is essential to the success of your trekking adventure. You rely on dialogue for the duration of the adventure: from planning to the

DOI: 10.4324/9781003586241-5

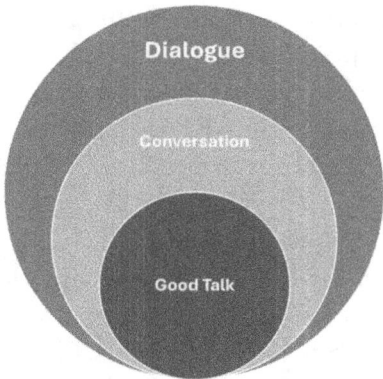

Figure 3.1 Types of Teacher-Friend Communication

trek, to traversing new or uncharted territories, to reaching your desired or surprise destination.

We endorse dialogue for your teacher-friend treks as a "culture of dialogue [that] challenges members of a community to create shared group norms that everyone buys into, to share their perspective openly and to invest in deepened and intentional relationship-building" (Ferdman & Graham, 2024, p. 21). In other words, we depend on dialogue to guide us through the adventure.

Dialogue

Dialogue is an intentional, intellectual, and inclusive way to share information and experiences. It centers discussion about related experiences, sets the stage for critical analysis of alternative viewpoints, and builds collective understanding. In fact, dialogue "is foundational to community engagement and learning across a range of settings" (Ferdman & Graham, 2024, p. 17). Let's examine the fundamental dimensions of dialogue.

First and foremost, dialogue is *intentional*. It is purpose-driven communication between people, in this case, teachers, who are seeking answers, exploring ideas, or satisfying a curiosity. We agree that "to engage in dialogue is one of the simplest ways … to cross boundaries…" (hooks, 1994, p. 130). As teacher-friends on a trek, dialogue might lead you to new places and take you to new spaces. It is central to self-directed learning or mutual mentoring experiences—creating "a space of empowerment and encouragement" (Nganga & Beck, 2017, p. 552) and reducing isolation. Though teaching is usually a solo endeavor, dialoguing about your practice invites others to know you and your teaching experiences. It opens classroom doors and shines a light on past and current pathways; it can illuminate future possibilities.

Second, dialogue is *intellectual* in nature; it is coherent and specific communication between people. Teachers, and mid-career teachers, in particular, have deep knowledge and extensive experience to exchange with one another. We think dialogue can be "rich descriptions of practice with careful and systematic interpretation of that practice" (Vanassche, 2023, p. 6). It can also include justifying talk (Vanassche, 2023) in which teacher-friends provide reasons or rationales for their actions.

Third, dialogue is *inclusive*. It is welcoming and ideally amplifies the voices of every person. In this inclusive and often empathetic type of communication, "everyone can show up as their full selves, feel seen and connect with one another more authentically" (Ferdman & Graham, 2024, p. 19). As such, genuine dialogue between teacher-friends requires mutual respect and trust. It also

> *... requires an intense faith in humankind, faith in their power to make and remake, to create and re-create, faith in their vocation to be more fully human (which is not the privilege of any elite, but the birthright of all).*
>
> (Freire, 2000, p. 92)

In other words, as trekking partners, you must have faith in one another for the duration of the journey.

Now, let's think about how dialogue supports your trekking adventure. During a trek, you:

- disclose knowledge of the terrain and elevation challenges,
- discuss basic needs and possible risks,
- negotiate an optimum pace for your trek, and
- strategize ways to handle the unexpected.

All these decisions influence your overall experience. Together, you and your partner, as teacher-friends, must communicate to not only survive but to thrive. Whether you are trekking in pairs or alone, consider the following ways you can tap into the power of dialogue.

Disclose Knowledge of Terrain and Elevation

As a mid-career teacher, you possess extensive tacit knowledge about schools and schooling. You know school structure can support teacher and student learning. Learning, after all, is situated and takes place within authentic activity, context, and culture (Lave & Wenger, 1991). Experienced teachers, like yourselves, are also keenly aware of how school organizational structures provide opportunities for working and learning together. Within these structures, you can engage in purposeful and productive dialogue.

We encourage teacher-friends as trekking partners to disclose what they know about their school's terrain—the formal organizational structures with one another. For example, you can reveal how to create pathways to teacher learning within your common planning time, professional learning communities, or critical friends' groups (Caskey & Carpenter, 2012). Such organizational structures often bring teachers with diverse backgrounds (e.g., ethnicity, gender, age, experience) and personalities together. You can work intentionally to ensure that each trekking partner has an opportunity to contribute.

We suggest that mid-career teachers can share what they know about ways to elevate or lower the intensity of their communication with another teacher. They already understand the importance of different levels of dialogue for different purposes. For example, teachers engage in higher levels of discourse when responding to a school crisis or an administrative directive, while they use lower levels of discourse when swapping stories about student antics or their personal experiences. All levels of dialogue are valuable and serve a purpose.

As you engage in dialogue with teacher-friends, you find ways to exchange what you know and believe in a considerate manner. You seek a certain rhythm, a type of balance, by sharing the time spent talking and listening, giving and receiving ideas, and voicing and hearing one another's concerns. Negotiating airtime is important for teacher-friends. After all, you are on this trekking adventure together.

Discuss Basic Needs and Possible Risks

Beyond exchanging knowledge about what is known about schools and schooling, you possess a tacit understanding of working together in a learning relationship. In this learning space, you can discuss what you need from a mutual mentoring relationship and your trepidations about investing in it. As experienced teachers, you can create mutually empowering relationships (Blake-Beard, n.d.) in which you learn and grow together.

What are the basic needs to consider when trekking with a teacher-friend? Basic needs may include having a thought partner who listens attentively and respectfully to your ideas, concerns, and aspirations about teaching with an open mind. Another example of a basic need is giving and receiving honest, objective, and constructive feedback when invited to do so. Similarly, dialogue can be a pathway for challenging and extending thinking, sharing and re-shaping understanding, and working collaboratively to create meaning (Nahmad-Williams & Taylor, 2015). Together, as teacher-friends, you share expectations and set boundaries for engaging in dialogue.

Yet, dialogue within this relational space is not without risks. Among the inherent risks are being misunderstood or not being heard. Other roadblocks to dialogue in learning relationships include *protective hesitation* (i.e., withholding critical feedback for fear of offending another person) and *protective defensiveness* (i.e., building personal walls to avoid critical feedback from another person) (Stanford University, 2019). Being aware of these possible risks and potential roadblocks is an important step in any trek.

Dialogue can reveal uncomfortable or unanticipated differences between you and your trekking partner. These differences do not need to become roadblocks to your interactions. Instead, we suggest accepting Ferdman and Graham's (2024) position:

> *Dialogue does not shy away from differences, but rather confronts and negotiates them directly, skillfully and respectfully. The ability to handle conflict of difficult conversations in educational, work and community settings is essential for everyone, and as such, is built over time.*
>
> (p. 19)

In other words, you can start small by taking short treks and discussing easy topics or more solvable problems. For example, you can take a short trek to talk about a new teaching strategy you are trying in your classroom, knowing your partner has reservations about it. Later, you and your partner can take longer treks as you build your learning relationship. For instance, you can swap stories about teaching dilemmas or challenges you are experiencing. You can also reserve longer treks for dialogue with teacher-friends you know well and believe can go the distance. For example, you can develop a yearlong plan for building equity-centered professional learning communities in your school. Such dialogue about practice is what can help propel you forward.

Negotiate an Optimum Pace

It is your trek, so you get to determine the pace of your trek, including the frequency and duration of dialogue. Teacher-friends can negotiate an optimum pace for their specific adventure. Together, they can decide how often and how long to engage in dialogue. For example, you may meet for 30 minutes once a week to discuss your immediate needs and meet monthly to delve into philosophical topics such as approaches to addressing student behavior, managing time, and planning career moves. Having a predetermined timeline (beginning and ending framework) helps to focus your dialogue—allowing time for slow, unhurried strolls or quick, hurried strides. Whether you choose a marathon, a sprint, or a modest pace, you and your partner ultimately get to decide the pace that works best for you and your trekking adventure.

Deciding the optimum pace is also important for a solo trekker. You get to determine the pace of your trek—how often and how long you engage in self-dialogue about your trekking adventure.

Strategize Ways to Handle the Unexpected

As teacher-friends, you also need to think about and plan for any unexpected hurdles you may encounter on your trek. Consider how you plan to move ahead despite the challenges. Will you go around, step over, or plow through the unanticipated obstacles along the path? Dialogue about how to handle rocky trail conditions or inclement weather is critical *before* you begin trekking.

Rocky trail conditions or inclement weather often take the form of interpersonal conflict, which occurs naturally when people interact (Hocker et al., 2022). When conflict does arise, you can be prepared to engage in respectful dialogue for exchanging perspectives in search of common ground. In fact, you can select a conflict resolution strategy such as accommodation (i.e., putting the other person's needs first), compromise (i.e., finding middle ground), or collaboration. Of these, collaboration is ideal.

> *To collaborate successfully, look at your conflict as a problem to solve together, not a competition to win individually. Flexibility also helps. You might think you've found the right answer, but your partner may have an idea that makes your solution even better.*
>
> (Raypole, 2020, "Collaboration" section)

In other words, as teacher-friends, you can use effective communication skills, including active listening and perspective taking, to reach "new ground" together.

Indeed, interpersonal communication is vital for any successful trek. Because "dialogue skills can help us be more nimble, flexible and thoughtful problem-solvers" (Ferdman & Graham, 2024, p. 19). What if you are on a solo trek? Let's look at self-dialogue for solo trekkers.

Self-dialogue

Self-dialogue can support your trekking adventure as well. Self-dialogue is a type of intrapersonal communication. It is an "internal dialogue between two subjects inside one's mind—between different parts of oneself or between oneself and the imagined partner" (Oleś et al., 2020, p. 2). For example, in an internal dialogue, you can pose questions about teaching practices and offer answers to those questions. As described by Fernyhough (2016), we dialogue with ourselves to prepare for, or reflect upon, our conversations with others.

According to Oleś et al. (2020), inner dialogues are types of *intrapersonal* communication between oneself or others (e.g., close friends, relatives, mentors). This type of self-dialogue allows you to take perspectives, gain understanding, and create representations of others' inner experiences. You may find yourself engaging in self-dialogue about your teaching practice as you drive to and from work. For instance, you may ruminate about troublesome classroom interactions as you leave school and have an inner dialogue about your emotional reactions. Then, the next morning, as you drive to work, you may review the troublesome interactions and rely on inner dialogue to consider alternative responses. We both recall having these inner dialogues with ourselves and our trusted others. Micki remembers having internal dialogues with her mother (a veteran teacher) as she struggled with managing interpersonal conflicts; Karen remembers having inner dialogues with another teacher (a mentor) as she worked to improve her practice.

In sum, dialogue and self-dialogue are useful for unpacking school and classroom experiences, considering alternative perspectives, and fostering understanding. Next, we delve into the power of conversation.

Conversation

Conversation, in our view, is informal communication between two or more people. During this type of exchange, teachers can report news, share thoughts, discuss ideas, and express feelings with one another. We also view conversation as "a source of nourishment" (Nhât Hạnh, 2013, p. 5). It creates a space for being together and "sharing the world" by "understanding and trusting the other" (van Manen, 2017, p. 818). We view it as a relational and social space in which teachers can speak, listen, or be silent depending on their personal and professional wishes. According to van Manen (2017), "sharing a true conversation can indeed offer valuable insight for … educators … or any professional for whom genuine conversations—the spoken words as well as the silences—constitute the main part of their professional practice" (p. 818). In other words, conversation is a common yet powerful type of communication for professional learning.

As a teacher, you already know that hallway conversations with a fellow teacher are invaluable. In these moments, you communicate information about school events (past, present, and future), describe rewarding or frustrating teaching experiences, and can express concerns about students (academic struggles, behavior, health, and well-being). These conversations may prompt you to act, reflect, or seek deeper dialogue with your trusted colleague.

We draw on ideas about engaging in conversations from the coaching conversations literature. According to Cheliotes and Reilly (2010), coaching conversations are:

- intentional,
- grounded in deep and meaningful listening, and
- candid.

Intentionality refers to seeking deep understanding, stronger relationships, and commitments to action. Grounded in deep and meaningful listening entails honoring others' perspectives and showing a willingness to be influenced by what others share. Being candid means speaking openly and honestly to build trust and interpersonal accountability. We think these ideas work well for any conversation between professionals like yourselves.

We find other key ideas from the coaching conversation literature about how to engage in conversations with your teacher-friends. For instance, the Center for Creative Leadership (2025) recommends:

1. Listen carefully to allow your partner to think, reflect, and express themselves. In other words, listen to understand.
2. Respond thoughtfully by asking powerful questions to clarify your partner's thinking and posing non-directive prompting questions to gain greater insight.
3. Resist imposing your own solution by shifting away from problem-solving, fixing, or giving advice.

The focus is on your partner's learning, not on your opinion or expertise. As some suggest, the art of conversation is finding an authentic mix of challenges and support to foster constructive dialogue.

As teacher-friends on a trek, conversations can help you to grapple with ideas and assumptions underlying teaching practices. Your trekking partner becomes a critical friend—one who not only encourages and supports you but also speaks honestly and constructively about issues with you. A critical friend asks hard questions, challenges your assumptions, and helps you tackle the most disorienting dilemmas. Collectively, you can forge a critical friendship that includes three characteristics:

- "a reciprocal, collaborative relationship
- a willingness to be challenged, and
- an intrinsically motivated willingness to engage in the relationship" (MacPhail et al., 2024, p. 600).

In sum, critical friendships rely on true conversations centered on personal goals and professional practice.

Interestingly, when you are trekking, you may discover that you do not always have to be talking; you can listen to your partner, note other sounds around you, or embrace the quiet. It is also worth noting that the conversations between teacher-friends need to be fluid.

Walking Conversations

Walking conversations "serve as a journey of sharing and listening, offering a space to consider our thoughts and feelings on pressing issues and to envision a positive future" (Reboot the Future, n.d., para. 4). These conversations are well suited and can be extremely valuable for teacher-friends who decide to go on a mutually rewarding trekking adventure. Let's explore some reasons for walking conversations.

David Baum (2018) explains why walking conversations work:

- When you are moving, you become more open. Your walking conversation can activate intuition and creativity because both your mind and body are engaged. "Body movement triggers bilateral brain functioning, which enables creativity and expansive thinking."
- Walking conversations move at a slower pace, which prompts *engagement* and *inclusion*. When you slow down your pace, you slow down your thinking, allowing you to consider another's ideas and point of view.
- Side-by-side or shoulder-to-shoulder conversations feel safer and less challenging than eye-to-eye or face-to-face conversations.
- Walking conversations have natural periods of silence as you look around and take steps along the path. Silence can create space for thinking (Baum, 2018, Why Walking Works section).

We agree with Baum's (2018) suggestion of taking a walk for your next critical conversation. As teacher-friends, you can begin (or continue) to tap the power of walking conversations.

Conversation among teachers is powerful, given its relational and social nature. Most teachers are adept at conversing with other teachers, administrators, students, and parents. Next, let's look at good talk and how teachers use it.

Good Talk

Good talk happens "between two people [trekkers] who share an affinity or attachment to one another not only to each other, but also to their shared world" (van Manen, 2014, p. 36). We view good talk as the intimate or heart work that happens among mid-career teachers as they consider common teaching challenges and seek opportunities for professional growth and change.

We agree that teachers benefit from "good talk about good teaching" to advance their professional practice (Palmer, 1993, p. 8). According to Palmer (1993), good topics for teachers' (i.e., university faculty) good talk are:

- "critical moments in teaching and learning
- the human condition of teachers and learners
- metaphors and images of what we are doing when we teach, and
- autobiographical reflection on the great teachers who helped bring us into academic life" (p. 10).

We think these topics are also relevant and appropriate for classroom teachers who wish to enhance their professional practice by engaging in good talk.

We also think good talk can include normalizing discourse (Vanassche, 2023). In the case of teacher-friends, normalizing discourse frames problems as typical or normal teaching issues (e.g., time management, classroom discipline). This type of talk plays an "important social function" (Vanassche, 2023, p. 5) for teachers who are navigating the ongoing demands and challenges of teaching in today's classrooms. Similarly, we think teachers use good talk to explain and validate (i.e., justify) their past, current, or anticipated actions with a trusted colleague.

Some scholars call for more focus on the role of professional talk in mentoring relationships. For instance, Becher and Orland-Barak (2018) reported:

Almost no research that we know of explores the contextual factors that mentors consider in their professional talk to inform and enact their practice. Such perspective can add a new angle to the study of context in mentoring by highlighting connections between social context and action through language. This invites a discursive stance to the study of mentoring, which focuses on **professional talk** *as reflective of how social and cultural environments inform mentors' thought and practice.*

(p. 479)

We contend that mutual mentoring between teacher-friends depends on good talk about their professional practice. Furthermore, we suggest that good talk works for trekking partners and solo trekkers alike. They can engage in good talk with themselves, known as self-talk.

Self-talk

Definitions of self-talk include "talk or thoughts directed at oneself" (Merriam-Webster, n.d.) and "self-directed or self-referent speech (either silent or aloud)" (Brinthaupt, 2019, para. 7). Self-talk serves self-regulatory functions such as:

- assisting with planning and regulating action,
- "keeping information in mind" about our supposed action, and
- "psyching ourselves up for action in the first place" (Fernyhough, 2016, p. 107).

In other words, self-talk helps to consciously articulate our experiences and thoughts before, during, and following our actions.

One powerful purpose of self-talk is affirmation. As mid-career teachers, you can use affirmations about what is working well in your classroom or school. For example, "I am a caring and competent teacher who treats my students and colleagues with respect." When on a trekking adventure, teacher-friends' affirmations may acknowledge openness to change. For instance, "We are working collaboratively and intentionally to learn more about AI and its implications for our classrooms." If trekking alone, the affirmation can also relate to professional growth. For example, "I am open-minded and eager to learn more about how my students are using AI." In each of these examples, self-talk centers on positive perceptions of self and related actions.

Hydration Station: Dialogue, Conversation, and Good Talk

You may be interested in reviewing what others say about dialogue, conversation, and good talk, including their value, and the role they play in self-directed learning (i.e., mentoring). Some say that "dialogue lives at the heart of supportive mentoring relationships" (Coombs & Goodwin, 2013, p. 59). Others say that dialogue with peers is a great way to learn about practice (Holland, 2018). We know that teacher-friends use dialogue to engage in purposeful discourse, exchange ideas, and pose questions about their teaching practice. They also converse frequently with one another and seek time to talk about their professional and personal lives. So, take a few moments to peruse the following findings and insights about dialogue, conversation, and good talk.

- Dialogue allows teachers in mentoring relationships to consider one another's personal philosophies about teaching, learning, and mentoring (Talbot et al., 2018).
- Patterns of mentoring dialogues include offering specific and non-specific feedback (positive and negative), discussing feedback,

asking questions and active listening, and initiating topics (Beek et al., 2019).
- Protocols can be valuable for guiding professional dialogues (Reinhardt et al., 2023; Windsor et al., 2022).
- Professional development needs to promote collegial dialogue within mentoring relationships and communities of practice (Hoekstra et al., 2018).
- "Positive reassurance, open communication, and collaborative planning … " are essential when holding critical conversations with teachers (Reinhardt et al., 2023, p. 7).
- Informal learning conversations facilitate positive relationships and "promote a stronger social bond" between teachers by connecting their teacher talk with social talk (Jones et al., 2023, p. 42).
- Teachers want opportunities to talk with and learn from other colleagues (Bressman et al., 2018).

Connecting to Practice

Mid-career teachers, like yourselves, are more confident and more comfortable with their teaching yet remain interested in exploring ways to deepen their practice and their students' learning experiences (Bressman et al., 2018). Dialogue, conversation, and good talk are all purposeful and practical ways for you to explore your professional practice. We believe these types of communication set the stage for mutually beneficial learning exchanges (i.e., mutual mentoring) in which teachers are "a mirror for one another to challenge assumptions … to grow individually because of investing in each other" (Swanson & Caskey, 2022, p. 9).

What does it take to be a mirror for one another? We think it requires a set of dispositions, including humility, gratitude, resilience, and intimacy. Let us explain each of these dispositions. Humility means adopting a stance of modesty or humbleness about yourself as a teacher and possessing an openness to growth. Gratitude means being grateful for or appreciative of the opportunity to engage in growth. Resilience means having strength and staying power while remaining flexible in your thinking and actions. (See Chapter 5 for more about teacher resilience.) Intimacy means having a sense of closeness or familiarity within a relationship. Whether you are trekking with a teacher-friend or trekking alone, these dispositions position you on a path for a successful trek toward personal and professional growth.

We think the following steps can help you connect dialogue, conversation, or good talk to your practice.

1. Choose a trekking partner. Basically, you have two choices: (a) select a teacher-friend to walk alongside, or (b) opt to walk alone.
2. Choose how you want to communicate. As described in this chapter, you need to pick the form of interpersonal communication that works best for you. Dialogue is ideal for mutual mentoring focused on professional learning to enrich or expand your teaching practice. Conversation works well for communicating about practice while taking walks, carpooling to/from school, or standing in school hallways. Good talk is perfect for exchanging thoughts and feelings within an existing community of practice (team, PLC, critical-friends group).
3. Choose a focus. You decide on the focus of your trekking adventure. Among the many focus areas, you may want to pick one related to professional growth (e.g., seeking new direction, revamping approach or strategy), building professional capacity (e.g., pursuing an advanced degree or webinar series, creating a new unit), or concentrating of mental health and well-being (e.g., handling stress, coping with burnout, dealing with dilemmas).
4. Choose a safe space for communication. You determine the best place for communicating with your trekking partner. Before or after school, you may want to meet in your classroom or school library. You may connect while walking or driving to and from school. During the school day, you may select a classroom, a conference room, or a quiet outdoor seating area. Similarly, you may opt to communicate while walking around the school grounds. Other times, you may wish to meet at a coffee shop, public library, or a teacher-friend's home.
5. Reflect on communication. As a teacher, you are continually reflecting on classroom or school experiences. Reflection after communication—whether engaging in dialogue, conversation, or good talk with a teacher-friend—or engaging in self-dialogue or self-talk—is invaluable. You can reap personal and professional benefits by taking time to ponder, contemplate, and wonder.

Keeping a Journal Revisited

We think that depth often comes with writing, more so than when responding orally. Writing tends to be deeper, more thoughtful, and more articulate; it may be beautiful. You are also making a commitment when putting your words, your ideas, thoughts, and feelings on paper. While we explain more about the power and purpose of keeping a journal in Chapter 2, we also wish to describe two ways of using a journal.

Solo work. You can use a journal for documenting and reflecting on your personal and professional growth. This type of journal offers you opportunities to write about your practice. Whether you are trekking with a partner or trekking alone, you can use this type of journal to focus on your teaching practice. In either case, you are investing time and thought by doing important solo work (self-talk). You are writing for yourself.

Partner work. Second, you can use a journal for dialogue with a teacher-friend. This type of journal is a tool for the written exchange of ideas. For mid-career teachers, a dialogue journal can prompt collaboration, exploration of ideas, problematizing issues, or enhancing teaching practice. When writing in a dialogue journal, you not only communicate your thinking, but you also get to review your written thoughts. After reading your teacher-friend's dialogue journal, you get to respond to their thoughts in any number of ways: reaction, question, confirmation, suggestion, and so on. This allows you to capture your dialogue in writing and interact socially with a peer, which we know is important for learning. You are writing for yourself and your trekking partner.

Conclusion

As teacher-friends, you have choices when it comes to engaging in dialogue, conversation, and good talk. Not only do you choose a format for communication, but you also get to choose whether your talks are positive or negative in nature. While we suggest it is best to frame communication positively, sometimes you may find yourself discussing negative experiences. For instance, you may engage in venting (letting off steam) about an interaction, or you may be complaining about an issue. In either instance, the purpose of such communication is to identify/clarify the problem and envision possible solutions. Ultimately, your dialogue, conversation, and good talk propel you to cover new ground.

Trail Talk

This chapter focuses on talking with one another—good talk. It is important to allow conversations to flow, but it is also important for mentoring conversations to be constructive. In today's trail talk, we invite you to discuss some of the following prompts to guide and build your mentoring relationship.

- How much time do we give to "venting," and what is our cue to switch to our trekking focus?
- How do you want to be told that you have "wandered off the trail"? As critical friends, it is important to redirect or refocus on one another so that our time together is productive.
- What topics are we interested in pursuing? Curriculum, pedagogy, behavior management, parent management, etc and so on.
- How do we want to organize our work? Create an agenda, free flow with a monthly review and planning session, or other ideas.

References

Baum, D. (2018, February 4). *The power of walking conversations.* https://www.davidbaum.com/news/2018/2/4/the-power-of-walking-conversations

Becher, A., & Orland-Barak, L. (2018). Context matters: Contextual factors informing mentoring in art initial teacher education. *Journal of Teacher Education, 69*(5), 477–492. https://doi.org/10.1177/0022487117720388

Beek, G. J., Zuiker, I., & Zwart, R. C. (2019). Exploring mentors' roles and feedback strategies to analyze the quality of mentoring dialogues. *Teaching and Teacher Education, 78*, 15–27. https://doi.org/10.1016/j.tate.2018.10.006

Blake-Beard, S. (n.d.). *Mentoring: Creating mutually empowering relationships.* https://womensleadership.stanford.edu/resources/voice-influence/mentoring-creating-mutually-empowering-relationships

Bressman, S., Winter, J. S., & Efron, S. E. (2018). Next generation mentoring: Supporting teachers beyond induction. *Teaching and Teacher Education, 73*, 162–170. https://doi.org/10.1016/j.tate.2018.04.003

Brinthaupt, T. M. (2019). Individual differences in self-talk frequency: Social isolation and cognitive disruption. *Frontiers in Psychology, 10*, 1088–1088. https://doi.org/10.3389/fpsyg.2019.01088

Caskey, M. M., & Carpenter, J. (2012). Organizational models for teacher learning. *Middle School Journal, 43*(5), 52–62. https://doi.org/10.1080/00940771.2012.11461830

Center for Creative Leadership. (2025). *How to have a coaching conversation.* https://www.ccl.org/articles/leading-effectively-articles/how-to-have-a-coaching-conversation/

Cheliotes, L. G., & Reilly, M. F. (2010). *Coaching conversations: Transforming your school one conversation at a time.* Corwin.

Coombs, D., & Goodwin, K. (2013). Give them something to talk about: The role of dialogue in mentoring relationships. *English Journal, 102*(3), 58–64. https://doi.org/10.58680/ej201322134

Ferdman, M., & Graham, F. (2024). The promise of building bridges. *Learning for Justice, 6*, 17–21.

Fernyhough, C. (2016). *The voices within: The history and science of how we talk to ourselves.* Basic Books.

Freire, P. (2000). *Pedagogy of the oppressed* (30th anniversary ed.). Continuum.

Hocker, J. L., Berry, K., & Wilmot, W. W. (2022). *Interpersonal conflict* (11th ed.). McGraw Hill.

Hoekstra, A., Kuntz, J., & Newton, P. (2018). Professional learning of instructors in vocational and professional education. *Professional Development in Education, 44*(2), 237–253. https://doi.org/10.1080/19415257.2017.1280523

Holland, E. (2018). Mentoring communities of practice: What's in it for the mentor? *International Journal of Mentoring and Coaching in Education, 7*(2), 110–126. https://doi.org/10.1108/IJMCE-04-2017-0034

hooks, b. (1994). *Teaching to transgress: Education as the practice of freedom.* Routledge. https://doi.org/10.4324/9780203700280

Jones, L., Tones, S., & Foulkes, G. (2023). Talking the talk: Dialogic mentoring in physical education. *Journal of Physical Education, Recreation & Dance, 94*(5), 40–45. https://doi.org/10.1080/07303084.2023.2185328

Lave, J., & Wenger, E. (1991). *Situated learning: Legitimate peripheral participation.* Cambridge University Press.

MacPhail, A., Tannehill, D., & Ataman, R. (2024). The role of the critical friend in supporting and enhancing professional learning and development. *Professional Development in Education, 50*(4), 597–610. https://doi.org/10.1080/19415257.2021.1879235

Merriam-Webster. (n.d.). Self-talk. In *Merriam-Webster.com dictionary*. Retrieved November 15, 2024, from https://www.merriam-webster.com/dictionary/self-talk

Nahmad-Williams, L., & Taylor, C. A. (2015). Experimenting with dialogic mentoring: A new model. *International Journal of Mentoring and Coaching in Education, 4*(3), 184–199. https://doi.org/10.1108/IJMCE-04-2015-0013

Nganga, C. W., & Beck, M. (2017). The power of dialogue and meaningful connectedness: Conversations between two female scholars. *The Urban Review, 49*(4), 551–567. https://doi.org/10.1007/s11256-017-0408-y

Nhât Hạnh, T. (2013). *The art of communicating.* HarperCollins Publishers.

Oleś, P. K., Brinthaupt, T. M., Dier, R., & Polak, D. (2020). Types of inner dialogues and functions of self-talk: Comparisons and implications. *Frontiers in Psychology, 11*(Article 227), 1–10. https://doi.org/10.3389/fpsyg.2020.00227

Palmer, P. J. (1993). Good talk about good teaching: Improving teaching through conversation and community. *Change: The Magazine of Higher Learning, 25*(6), 8–13. https://doi.org/10.1080/00091383.1993.9938466

Raypole, C. (2020). *How to handle interpersonal conflict like a pro.* https://www.healthline.com/health/interpersonal-conflict

Reboot the Future. (n.d.). *Walking conversations.* https://www.rebootthefuture.org/articles/walking-conversations

Reinhardt, K. S., Lynch-Davis, K., & Johnson, R. D. (2023). Strengthening critical conversations in the teacher residency: Mentor professional development. *SRATE Journal, 32*(2), 1–9.

Stanford University. (2019). *Mentoring: Creating mutually empowering relationships* [Discussion guide]. VMware Women's Leadership Innovation Lab. https://womensleadership.stanford.edu/node/796/mentoring-creating-mutually-empowering-relationships

Swanson, K. W., & Caskey, M. M. (2022). Mentoring dialogue and practice: A transformative experience. *Journal of Transformative Learning, 9*(1), 8–17.

Talbot, D., Denny, J., & Henderson, S. (2018). 'Trying to decide ... what sort of teacher I wanted to be': Mentoring as a dialogic practice. *Teaching Education, 29*(1), 47–60. https://doi.org/10.1080/10476210.2017.1347919

Vanassche, E. (2023). Talking to learn: Patterns of discursive interaction in post-lesson debriefs. *Teaching and Teacher Education, 133,* 104301. https://doi.org/10.1016/j.tate.2023.104301

van Manen, M. (2014). *Phenomenology of practice: Meaning-giving methods in phenomenological research and writing.* Left Coast Press. https://doi.org/10.4324/9781315422657

van Manen, M. (2017). Phenomenology in its original sense. *Qualitative Health Research, 27*(6), 810–825. https://doi.org/10.1177/1049732317699381

Windsor, S., Kriewaldt, J., Nash, M., Lilja, A., & Thornton, J. (2022). Developing teachers: Adopting observation tools that suspend judgement to stimulate evidence-informed dialogue during the teaching practicum to enrich teacher professional development. *Professional Development in Education, 48*(4), 642–656. https://doi.org/10.1080/19415257.2020.1712452

4

Practice

Going Deeper and Moving Forward

We view practice as a way of doing, thinking about, and being in the teaching profession. Although some define practice as what people do, we agree with Grossman et al. (2009) that practice also extends to who people are and how they think. Certainly, in our profession, practice includes procedures, routines, and understandings related to teaching in schools. But our practice also includes who we are (i.e., teachers) and how we think (e.g., reflective).

Others describe practice in terms of "its goals, its activities, and its historical traditions … that been developed over time by others…" (Grossman et al., 2009, p. 2059). For instance, those pursuing the field of medicine may be entering medical practice. Yet, others refer to practice as a usual way of doing something, such as yoga practice or writing practice.

Teaching practice, likewise, is complex and ever-changing. While we acknowledge that practice includes specific teaching skills or competencies, we also assert that practice extends beyond the classroom and serves as mirrors for challenging one another's assumptions (Weller Swanson & Caskey, 2021). Learning the complexities and nuances of practice helps us to become better teachers (Swanson & Caskey, 2024).

We hold a broad view of teaching given its complex and nuanced nature. As Loughran (2013) articulated so clearly:

> *Teaching then is not bound by a script or set of routines but depends on a teacher making informed decisions about practice. From this perspective, teaching is dynamic and demanding because it must be responsive to the varied learning demands inherent in the situation. Seeing practice*

DOI: 10.4324/9781003586241-6

> *in this way means it must be understood as problematic because narrow views of teaching and learning only serve to mask this complexity.*
>
> (p. 120)

In other words, the practice of teaching requires a deep understanding of the evolving and complicated interplay of teaching and learning.

During our teaching careers, we had opportunities to learn from other teachers. We also read widely and came to embrace the wisdom of some of education's greatest thinkers.

- First, we agree with Noddings' (2003) position that "teaching qualifies as a practice if not a profession" (p. 247). Teaching is a practice and a profession.
- Second, we accept Shulman's (1998) and Noddings' (2003) stance about the educator's responsibility to others. Shulman asserts that practitioners, as members of a profession, have a responsibility to their colleagues and clients. More specifically, Nodding contends that schoolteachers accept some responsibility for developing students as whole people.
- Third, we recognize the distinction between theory and practice. In this thoughtful work about the phenomenon of practice, van Manen (1997) suggests that theory "thinks" the world, whereas practice "grasps" the world. Later, he explains that practice encompasses a sense of oneself as well as "relational perceptiveness, tact for knowing what to say and do in contingent situations, thoughtful routines and practices, and other aspects of knowledge…" (van Manen, 2007, p. 20).
- Fourth, we subscribe to Grossman et al.'s (2009) idea that practice involves the identity of the practitioner. In the teaching profession, "practitioners use aspects of their own personalities, as well as their professional identities, as an intimate part of their practice" (Grossman et al., 2009, p. 2059). Teachers, in other words, bring themselves into their teaching practice.

We offer these big ideas about practice as a backdrop for the following sections that focus on features of practice, engaging in practice, and supporting practice through dialogue. Let's start by looking at some key features of teacher practice.

Key Features of Teacher Practice

In this section, we cover valuable terrain associated with practice. While not an exhaustive trek, we consider three essential features: pedagogy, relationships, and collaboration.

Pedagogy: Teaching and Learning

Pedagogy is at the core of practice. According to Loughran (2013), "Pedagogy is about the teaching–learning relationship" (p. 135); it is a complex and generative part of practice. Experienced teachers, like you, understand that teaching and learning are active and ongoing processes in the classroom. Thus, we position pedagogy at the core of practice.

Central to pedagogy is the idea of *noticing*. As described by Mason (2002), noticing requires teachers to (a) be present and sensitive to the moment, (b) have reason to act, and (c) have a different act come to mind (p. 1). Typically, teachers' noticing focuses on how students are learning. Loughran (2013) summarized that teachers:

> ... needed to be conscious of the interactions between teaching and learning in the real time of classroom practice ... teachers were doing more than looking into their teaching; they were actually beginning to be aware of, and responsive to the overall pedagogical experience, not only as it was conceptualized in planning but also as it was unfolding in practice.
>
> (p. 121)

In other words, teachers have the opportunity to learn from and respond to their teaching experience as it unfolds in their classrooms.

Teachers invite their whole selves into the teaching and learning process. While connecting their pedagogical knowledge and practice, they bring their teacher selves and personalities (Carmi, 2024). According to hooks (1994), "Teaching is a performative act. And it is that aspect of our work that offers the space for change, invention, spontaneous shifts, that can serve as a catalyst drawing out the unique elements in each classroom" (p. 11). We love hooks' (1994) stance about how teaching can serve as a catalyst—"a catalyst that calls everyone to become more and more engaged, to become active participants in learning" (p. 11). In other words, we do not leave parts of ourselves in the hallway. We bring whole selves into the classroom, and we allow our students to do the same.

Seasoned teachers, like you, remain attuned to how teaching creates a space for drawing out the best in students. You focus on the joy of teaching and learning with your students. Why? Because you want to make a difference in the lives of the students you teach. Your care for another (student or peer) is "fundamental to teaching as a practice" (Noddings, 2003, p. 247). As expressed so eloquently by Noddings (2003), "To teach in a manner that respects and cares for the souls of our students is essential if we are to provide the necessary conditions where learning can most deeply and intimately begin" (p. 13). Holding onto these core beliefs (i.e., making a difference and caring) can help you navigate the bumpy trails you encounter while teaching.

As you create spaces for learning, you are continually making pedagogical decisions about your practice. According to Loughran (2013), "teachers' active decision making and the reasoning that directs and informs their practice has a great deal to do with the ways in which teaching and learning experiences unfold in the practice setting" (p. 120). In other words, teachers are continually making "in the moment" decisions about their teaching. In fact, teachers make decisions a day, which may result in decision fatigue. Engaging in dialogue, conversation, or good talk with a teacher-friend can help you to grapple with the ideas and assumptions underlying your decisions.

Relationships: Students, Colleagues, and Self

Relationships are at the heart of practice. First, let's consider relationships with students. As noted by Noddings (2003):

> *Teaching is thoroughly relational, and many of its goods are relational: the feeling of safety in a thoughtful teacher's classroom, a growing intellectual enthusiasm in both teacher and student, the challenge and satisfaction shared by both in engaging new material, the awakening sense (for both) that teaching and life are never-ending moral quests.*
>
> (p. 249)

In other words, practice is about relationships with students. You affect the lives of students not just by what you teach but by how you relate to them. Your relationships with them make a difference. As teachers, you are in a moral contract with students, who are watching and waiting for us to build honest relationships with them (Sizer & Sizer, 1999). As experienced teachers, you already know that the keys to building honest relationships with students start with showing genuine interest in their welfare, recognizing their academic and social needs, honoring their contributions, and respecting their perspectives.

Second, practice is about our relationships with colleagues. In our profession, you can build relationships with other teachers by revealing who you are, sharing your successes and frustrations, and unpacking your assumptions. In doing so, you may find opportunities for personal and professional growth as well as deeper connections with your colleagues. Building and sustaining these relationships makes traveling uncharted territories less daunting and certainly less isolating. Many schools already have organizational models (e.g., professional learning communities, critical friends groups) that foster collegial relationships (Caskey & Carpenter, 2012). Whether your school has such models or not, you can build a positive and productive learning relationship with a teacher-friend.

Third, practice includes a relationship with one's self. While sometimes overlooked, teachers' relationship with themselves is fundamental to practice.

In discussing the phenomenology of practice, van Manen (2007) points to the importance of the formative relations of "being and acting" and "who we are and how we act" (p. 15). In other words, we cannot separate who we are from how we act. Others also emphasize this relationship. As Parker Palmer (1998) insists, "we teach who we are" (p. 1). We share this overarching belief that you teach who you are, so you must have a wholesome relationship with yourself. (See Chapter 3 about the importance of self-talk as a means to foster a positive relationship with yourself.)

Collaboration

Collaboration is the soul of practice. As experienced teachers, you know that today's school climate depends on teacher collaboration. Together, you tackle not only the day-to-day challenges associated with teaching (e.g., meeting students' individual academic, social, and emotional needs) but also the larger, critical issues troubling school environments (e.g., homelessness, substance use). It may come as no surprise that collaboration among teachers contributes to improvements in student achievement and teacher practice (Ronfeldt et al., 2015).

Collaboration can also nurture teacher collegiality and reduce teacher isolation. In fact, "[T] teachers' overall work-life can improve with high levels of common planning time" (Caskey & Carpenter, 2012, p. 54) because it affords them a time and place for collaboration within the school day. Teacher collaboration takes place in multiple ways, including team, department, and grade-level meetings. Teacher collaboration during regular teacher hours is invaluable and can occur within professional learning communities and critical friends' groups (Caskey & Carpenter, 2012).

As an experienced teacher, you know that collaboration takes time. You need time to collaborate with fellow teachers and other school personnel. This allocation of collaborative time extends to time for professional learning as well as time for professional and personal renewal. Thus, as research confirms, schools need to allocate time for collaboration within teachers' contract hours (Caskey & Carpenter, 2012; Davis & Chick, 2022; Ronfeldt et al., 2015). Not only does time foster collaboration, but it also relates to teachers' overall well-being, as we discuss in the next section.

Engaging in Practice

Of course, engaging in practice is what you do as teachers. Yet, we believe teachers want to derive some personal and professional benefit from engaging in their practice. Thus, we agree with Palmer (1998), who posited:

If we want to grow in our practice, we have two primary places to go: To the inner ground from which good teaching comes, and to the community of fellow teachers from whom we can learn more about ourselves and our craft.

(p. 141)

So, how do we start? We begin by looking at three hallmarks: reflection, personal and professional well-being, and intentional self-care.

Reflection

As an experienced teacher, you know that teaching is rarely a solitary endeavor. Every instructional day, students are all around you—in the classroom, hallways, and common areas. You interact with fellow teachers, school staff, administrators, and parents. So, your teaching practice demands your full attention and offers few moments of "down time." Despite this total immersion in teaching, you are continually thinking about your practice. In fact, you are likely already tapping the power of reflecting on your teaching—either in the moment or at a future point in time.

Reflection is the process of engaging in reflective practice; it positions you as a researcher of your own practice. According to Schön (1983), as a practitioner, you become a "researcher in the practice context" (p. 68). In other words, you study your own practice. You think and act in response to a problem, surprise, confusion, or inconsistency in your teaching (Shepherd, 2006). As explained by Boud (2001), reflection after an experience gives you the opportunity to (a) return to the experience, (b) attend to feelings, and (c) reevaluate the experience. Reflective inquiry is one of the most important aspects of professional learning (Gut et al., 2016).

Reflective practice also helps you to understand the nature of your practice. It can provide you with an opportunity to analyze teaching routines, approaches, or strategies, so you can reproduce or improve them (Gut et al., 2016). You can also use a journal to capture your thoughts and feelings about your practice. According to Shepherd (2006), a reflective journal "casts a spotlight on practice," allowing you to see and be a witness to your practice and be in a "better position to improve it" (p. 338). The first step is to articulate what you do. Furthermore, a reflective journal can be used to prompt self-reflection and serve as a starting point for engaging in dialogue, conversation, or good talk with other teachers.

Well-being

Teacher well-being is an essential yet possibly overlooked dimension of practice. What is teacher-well-being? Teacher well-being includes a sense of personal and professional fulfillment, satisfaction, purposefulness, and happiness constructed in collaboration with colleagues and students (Soini et al., 2010). While teachers, administrators, school staff, parents, and communities attend to student well-being, who is attending to teacher well-being? Research shows that "the teacher community plays an important part in teachers' occupational well-being" (Soini et al., 2010, p. 746). Teachers emphasize the importance of emotional support from other teachers and a positive school atmosphere for their overall well-being.

Teacher wellness "directly influences the wellness and performance of students. Teachers will be able to perform better in their classrooms if they have the occupational resources needed to sustain their work. This in turn could lead to better student performance" (Fiereck et al., 2016, p. 56). In other words, teacher well-being relates to student success. In contrast, when teachers experience high levels of stress, they are less able to perform their teaching duties or may miss more instructional days (Fiereck et al., 2016). They may experience emotional exhaustion leading to teacher burnout (Tantillo Philibert et al., 2020). Focusing on teachers' wellness can help lower teachers' stress levels and improve their overall work-life. Furthermore, attending to teacher well-being is a major teacher retention strategy (Davis & Chick, 2022).

As you might expect or predict, teachers also need to attend to their own well-being across their career span. Based on their recent research, Davis and Chick (2022) concluded, "Teachers must actively address their social, emotional, physical, and psychological well-being throughout their careers" (p. 7). How do we suggest you actively address your well-being? We recommend two complementary approaches. First, engage in dialogue, conversation, or good talk with a teacher-friend to discuss thoughts and feelings about your well-being. Second, attend to self-care, which happens to be the topic of our next section.

Self-care

Self-care needs to be an essential ingredient in your practice. As an experienced teacher, you must take care of yourself before you care for your students or colleagues. Remember that you need to put on your oxygen mask before you help others with theirs. For practitioners, self-care is a "nonnegotiable necessity" (Gill Lopez, 2020, p. 79); it is "not narcistic or selfish, but an act of self-respect" (Gill Lopez, 2020, 78). Self-care is an absolute priority for school professionals to be at their best and for students to thrive.

What is self-care? According to Lopez (2017), self-care is "the intentional, proactive pursuit of integrated wellness through balancing mind, body, and spirit personally and professionally" (p. 2). What does she mean by intentional, proactive, integrated, and balanced?

- Intentional means to do something deliberately. It is a purposeful, premeditated act.
- Proactive means to be preemptive (doing something before it has to be done).
- Integrated means caring for and functioning as a whole person.
- Balance means to attend to all aspects of the person (mind, body, spirit) with equal frequency (Lopez, 2017, p. 2).

As others explain, self-care relies on knowledge of self and checking in with oneself to see what we need at a given time (Cleantis, 2017). Self-care is necessary to counter the effects of stress and potential professional burnout. We also know that self-care can be temporary and enduring (Gill Lopez, 2020). Let's look at both kinds of self-care.

Temporary
Temporary self-care refers to engaging in activities that "release hormones and neurotransmitters that produce positive feelings" (National Association of School Psychologists [NASP], 2021, p. 2). These activities are typically brief, relaxing, or enjoyable ones that grant you some space, create a sense of peace, or lift your mood. They are temporary in nature as the positive feelings fade after the activity ends. Examples of temporary self-care activities include exercise (releases endorphins), eating and sleeping well (releases serotonin), going out to dinner with a friend (releases oxytocin), or watching a movie or reading a book (releases dopamine) (NASP, 2021).

Enduring
Enduring self-care involves long-term practices and habits that strengthen our neurological functioning. These practices include a "mindfulness component that exercises the phenomenon of neuroplasticity to change the physical structure of the brain" (NASP, 2021, p. 2). According to Kabat-Zinn (2015), "mindfulness can be thought of as moment-to-moment, nonjudgmental awareness, cultivated by paying attention in a specific way, that is, in the present moment, and as non-reactively, as non-judgmentally, and as open-heartedly as possible" (p. 1481). In other words, mindfulness helps us be more fully aware. Notably, mindfulness is self-care that keeps giving beyond the moment because it restructures our thinking in ways that result in more focused attention and self-regulation (NASP, 2021). Examples of enduring self-care practices include taking time to do something for yourself, meeting regularly with a friend, keeping a gratitude journal, and building in routines (daily or weekly) that bring you joy.

Our focus on self-care is not unique to K–12 education. Complementary professions are touting the value of self-care and offering ideas for incorporating self-care practices. In social work, scholars note the efficacy of self-care practices for educators who are seeking to improve their professional well-being and overall health (Davis & Chick, 2022; Lee et al., 2020). The National Association for School Psychologists (NASP, 2021), on a similar path, suggests how schools can prioritize self-care and build a kinder, gentler space for learning. For example, schools can:

- provide intentional teaching and learning opportunities (i.e., professional development), and
- embed regular self-care practices into school life (e.g., a minute of breathing at the start of the day for the entire school, a minute of breathing for school personnel at the beginning of meetings).

Because it has pragmatic, meaningful, and potentially long-lasting benefits, we endorse self-care as a critical practice for teachers. Whether you are trekking with a partner (e.g., teacher-friend), partners (e.g., community of practice), or alone, you must take care of yourself.

Supporting Practice through Dialogue

Dialogue is an effective and readily available way for teachers to support their practice (Chapter 3). Through dialogue about practice, teachers like you can engage in discussion and exchange ideas for deepening understanding, building new knowledge, and growing professionally. These interactions can help teachers not only make sense of their current practice (Swanson & Caskey, 2022) but can also shape future practice.

Practice is a major part of teachers' professional work. Another part is professional development in the workplace. According to Dall'Alba and Sandberg (2006), the workplace must encourage discussions to advance one's own understanding of what practice involves and gain exposure to other understandings of practice. Then, professionals need to critically consider, evaluate, and possibly challenge and extend understandings. In the teaching profession, teachers are continually making decisions and thinking about their practice. Having discussions with a trekking partner or teacher-friend can encourage both to grapple with ideas and assumptions that underlie decisions and inform practice.

To support your practice with dialogue, you can engage with another teacher as *critical friends* or with multiple teachers in *communities of practice*. You can also support your practice by engaging in dialogue using *critical reflection*.

Critical Friends

Critical friends are trusted people who provide constructive feedback and support to help improve a person's practice. In education, critical friends play a valuable role in professional learning (MacPhail et al., 2024). In "highly tailored" professional development, a critical friend can contribute to growth by "providing support and stimulating reflection and challenging educators to continuously develop their knowledge and skills" (MacPhail et al., 2024, p. 599). A critical friend can also influence professional growth within a mentoring relationship. In any case, critical friends need to build a high-quality relationship with one another—one built on mutual respect and trust.

We envision teacher-friends as critical friends. As critical friends, you must invest considerable time to create a critical friendship and a reciprocal relationship. According to MacPhail et al. (2024), "critical friendship always has three defining characteristics:

- a reciprocal, collaborative relationship,
- a willingness to be challenged, and
- an intrinsically motivated willingness to engage in the relationship (p. 600)."

A critical friend relationship takes time to build and positions you to "interrogate and improve each other's respective philosophies and practices" (MacPhail et al., 2024, p. 608). As you start your trekking journey about practice, consider choosing a path to traverse alongside a teacher-friend.

Communities of Practice

Communities of practice are groups of people (e.g., experienced teachers) who share a passion for doing something (e.g., teaching) and want to deepen their understanding and expertise of practice by belonging to the group (e.g., teacher-friends, trekking partners). These communities enhance and strengthen opportunities for professional learning about practice. We believe communities can serve to engage mid-career teachers with the ebb and flow of growing as professionals (Swanson & Caskey, 2024).

Communities of practice have three characteristics: mutual engagement, a joint enterprise, and a shared repertoire (Wenger, 1998). Briefly, *mutual engagement* refers to how members engage in practice and negotiate what practice means with each other. For example, mid-career teachers talking with other teachers who have different experiences may help bring more coherence to their teaching practice. *Joint enterprise* is how members navigate the complexity of their mutual engagement. For instance, mid-career teachers are unearthing ways to collaborate despite their individual differences in response to local teaching demands or challenges. *Shared repertoire* denotes the range and collection of ways to mutually engage and negotiate meaning in practice. For illustration, mid-career teachers draw upon common terminology, concepts, histories or experiences, perspectives, routines, and actions serving as resources for their practice.

We believe that a community of practice can be a fertile ground for teachers mentoring teachers. Together, they can discuss teaching, exchange ideas, explore options, collaborate on initiatives, and more (Swanson & Caskey, 2024). Mentoring refers to a "relationship between individuals," whereas communities of practice include a "full set of relations (i.e., persons and activities) within a particular social context (i.e., community)" (Bottoms et al., 2020, p. 146). We contend that mentoring within communities of practice can nurture a dynamic flow of knowledge and foster reciprocity among mid-career teachers that benefits the entire community.

Critical Reflection

Another way to support practice using dialogue is through critical reflection. According to Brookfield (1998):

> *Critically reflective practice is a process of inquiry involving practitioners in trying to discover, and research, the assumptions that frame how they work. Critically reflective practitioners constantly research these assumptions by seeing practice through four complementary lenses: the lens of their own autobiographies as learners of reflective practice, the lens of learners' eyes, the lens of colleagues' perceptions, and the lens of theoretical, philosophical, and research literature.*
>
> (p. 197)

As experienced teachers, you can use these lenses to give you four different ways to look at what you do. Further, tapping into these four lenses can be "pedagogically helpful, emotionally necessary, and politically significant" (Brookfield, 2017, p. 95). For more details about each of the four lenses, walk over to Chapter 6.

As a mid-career teacher, you may already be engaged in critically reflective practice. You may also be curious about the many advantages of engaging in critical reflection. As listed by Brookfield (2017), critical reflection can help teachers to:

- take informed action,
- develop a rationale for practice,
- the emotional roller coaster of teaching,
- avoid "self-laceration" (blaming self when student if students are not learning),
- enlivens the classroom,
- keep engaged,
- model democratic values, and
- increase trust (pp. 202–204).

You may also decide to tap students' eyes using Brookfield's (1998) *Critical Incident Questionnaire* (CIQ). Reasons you may wish to use a CIQ include:

- alerting you to problems that need addressing,
- grounding your actions in accurate information,
- developing students' reflectivity,
- building trust between you and your students,
- justifying your use of diverse teaching methods,
- modeling critical thinking,
- displaying your responsiveness to students' opinions, and
- highlighting democratic principles (Brookfield, 1998).

In other words, as a critically reflective teacher, you gain a wider perspective by seeking and honoring students' input.

Hydration Station: Practice

We know that you, as mid-career teachers, possess considerable tacit knowledge about practice. However, you may want to know more about the practice shared in recent publications of researchers' findings and practitioners' thinking. In addition, you may discover that your experiences and thinking align with other educators' thoughts.

- "Practice in complex domains involves the orchestration of understanding, skill, relationship, and identity to accomplish particular activities with others in specific environments" (Grossman et al., 2009, p. 2059).
- "…teaching is a relational practice—one that has its own distinctive criteria of internal excellence" (Noddings, 2003, p. 251).

- "We must observe each other teach, at least occasionally—and we must spend more time talking to each other about teaching" (Palmer, 1998, p. 143).
- Ronfeldt et al. (2015) shared that "85% of teachers in their study identified as being a part of 'a team or group of colleagues that works together on instruction' and report that collaboration in these teams is quite extensive and helpful" (p. 512).
- "...the interactive features of the practice may be visible, but the professional reasoning underlying the practitioners' actions may be invisible" (Grossman et al., 2009, p. 2066).
- "....rather than progressing through time, teachers may develop their skills and practice in a non-linear fashion" (Booth et al., 2021, p. 8).
- Professional development needs to be collaborative and engaging, and provide opportunities for teachers to improve their practice in meaningful ways (Davis & Chick, 2022).
- Mid-career teachers expect autonomy in directing their classroom instruction. They believe it is possible to influence the content of professional development and how it is put into practice (Gimbert & Kapa, 2022).
- Teacher mentoring about practice is not only multifaceted but may also promote professionalism (Carmi, 2024).

What thoughts and feelings did these statements evoke? Our hope is that you find some to be affirming, inspiring, or provocative.

Keeping a Journal

Keeping a journal, journaling, can be an invaluable way to document thinking and action related to learning experiences, professional and personal. You can use a journal to reflect on practice, pose questions for pondering, or capture ideas. Not only can you write your thoughts and express your feelings in a journal, but you can also reread your entries as you wish. Thus, a journal becomes a resource; tap it often to inform or explore your professional practice.

Teachers and scholars alike find value in journaling about their professional practice. For example, Shepherd (2006) shared how he wrote about an incident that interested or puzzled him as descriptively and objectively as possible. Then, he responded to four reflective questions related to the incident:

- How do I feel about this?
- What do I think about this?
- What have I learned from this?
- What action will I take as a result of my lessons learned?

Shepherd asserted that using reflective questions helped to "facilitate reflective thinking" and "make sense of the complexity" (p. 336). He was deliberately working to separate his thoughts and feelings about an incident. We encourage you to try Shepherd's (2006) approach or adapt it for your own reflective journal.

Conclusion

We view pedagogy (teaching and learning) as the core of your professional practice. As teachers, you focus on practice as you arrive at school, enter your classroom, and interact with peers. Not only does practice demand your ever-present attention during school hours, but it also infiltrates your thinking beyond the instructional day. We envision relationships at the heart of practice because teaching is a relational practice (Noddings, 2003). We see collaboration as the soul of practice and an essential aspect in teacher-friend mentoring relationships. Together, pedagogy, relationships, and collaboration are the inherent realities of practice.

Because we believe that practice requires attention, your personal and professional selves, we cast a spotlight on reflection, teacher well-being, and self-care. We suggest using critical friend groups, communities of practice, and critical reflection as powerful ways to create space for dialogue about practice. As you move forward on a trek—whether with a teacher-friend, small group, or alone—your personal outlook or mindset about professional learning comes into play. Remember to reserve space for transparency, risk-taking, creativity, reciprocity, and most importantly, hope.

Trail Talk

Time to engage in a trail talk about your practice. Consider the following conversation starters as you walk with a teacher-friend or trek alone. When thinking about your practice:

- What do you like and want to continue?
- What would you like to change, if you could?
- Where might you look for inspiration?
- What brings you joy?
- What gives you hope?

References

Booth, J., Coldwell, M., Müller, L.-M., Perry, E., & Zuccollo, J. (2021). Mid-career teachers: A mixed methods scoping study of professional development, career progression and retention. *Education Sciences, 11*(6), 299. https://doi.org/10.3390/educsci11060299

Bottoms, S. I., Pegg, J., Adams, A., Risser, H. S., & Wu, K. (2020). Mentoring within communities of practice. In B. J. Irby, J. N. Boswell, L. J. Searby, F. Kochan, R. Garza, & N. Abdelrahman (Eds.), *The Wiley international handbook of mentoring* (1st ed., pp. 141–166). Wiley. https://doi.org/10.1002/9781119142973.ch10

Boud, D. (2001). Using journal writing to enhance reflective practice. *New Directions for Adult and Continuing Education, 2001*(90), 9–18. https://doi.org/10.1002/ace.16

Brookfield, S. (1998). Critically reflective practice. *Journal of Continuing Education in the Health Professions, 18*(4), 197–205. https://doi.org/10.1002/chp.1340180402

Brookfield, S. D. (2017). *Becoming a critically reflective teacher* (2nd ed.). Jossey-Bass.

Carmi, T. (2024). Reframing high-quality mentoring: Between teacher mentoring and visions of teaching as a profession. *Journal of Teacher Education, 75*(2), 186–202. https://doi.org/10.1177/00224871231200276

Caskey, M. M., & Carpenter, J. (2012). Organizational models for teacher learning. *Middle School Journal, 43*(5), 52–62. https://doi.org/10.1080/00940771.2012.11461830

Cleantis, T. (2017). *An invitation to self-care: Why learning to nurture yourself is the key to the life you've always wanted. 7 principles for abundant living.* Simon and Schuster.

Dall'Alba, G., & Sandberg, J. (2006). Unveiling professional development: A critical review of stage models. *Review of Educational Research, 76*(3), 383–412. https://doi.org/10.3102/00346543076003383

Davis, B., & Chick, W. (2022). Self-care and self-advocacy for improved educator engagement and satisfaction: A guide for teachers and administrators. In K. L. Clarke (Ed.), *Advances in higher education and professional development* (pp. 1–23). IGI Global.

Fiereck, R., Hammerschmidt, E., Le, M., Lu, N., Traynor, C., & Wong, V. (2016). *Smart solutions to Minnesota's teacher shortage: Developing and sustaining a diverse and valued educator workforce.* Education Minnesota, Educator Policy Innovation Center. https://educationminnesota.org/wp-content/uploads/2021/08/EPIC-Recruitment-Retention-Report.pdf

Gill Lopez, P. (2020). Practitioner self-care: Mind–body best practice. In C. Maykel, & M. A. Bray (Eds.), *Promoting mind–body health in schools: Interventions for mental health professionals* (pp. 77–92). American Psychological Association. https://psycnet.apa.org/doi/10.1037/0000157-006

Gimbert, B. G., & Kapa, R. R. (2022). Mid-career teacher retention: Who Intends to stay, where, and why? *Journal of Education Human Resources, 40*(2), 228–265. https://doi.org/10.3138/jehr-2020-0037

Grossman, P., Compton, C., Igra, D., Ronfeldt, M., Shahan, E., & Williamson, P. W. (2009). Teaching practice: A cross-professional perspective. *Teachers College Record: The Voice of Scholarship in Education, 111*(9), 2055–2100. https://doi.org/10.1177/016146810911100905

Gut, D. M., Wan, G., Beam, P. C., & Burgess, L. (2016). Reflective dialog journals: A tool for developing professional competence in novice teachers. *School-University Partnerships, 9*(2), 60–70.

hooks, b. (1994). *Teaching to transgress: Education as the practice of freedom.* Routledge. https://doi.org/10.4324/9780203700280

Kabat-Zinn, J. (2015). Mindfulness. *Mindfulness, 6*(6), 1481–1483. https://psycnet.apa.org/doi/10.1007/s12671-015-0456-x

Lee, J. J., Miller, S. E., & Bride, B. E. (2020). Development and initial validation of the self-care practices scale. *Social Work, 65*(1), 21–28. https://doi.org/10.1093/sw/swz045

Lopez, P. G. (2017). Self-care: The missing link in best practice – Part II. *Communiqué, 45*(5), 1–8.

Loughran, J. (2013). Pedagogy: Making sense of the complex relationship between teaching and learning. *Curriculum Inquiry, 43*(1), 118–141. https://doi.org/10.1111/curi.12003

MacPhail, A., Tannehill, D., & Ataman, R. (2024). The role of the critical friend in supporting and enhancing professional learning and development. *Professional Development in Education, 50*(4), 597–610. https://doi.org/10.1080/19415257.2021.1879235

Mason, J. (2002). *Researching your own practice: The discipline of noticing.* RoutledgeFalmer.

National Association of School Psychologists [NASP]. (2021). *Evidence-based self-care practices to promote wellness and combat stress and burnout.* https://core-docs.s3.amazonaws.com/documents/asset/uploaded_file/3447/NRSD/2970196/Self_Care_Practives.pdf

Noddings, N. (2003). Is teaching a practice? *Journal of Philosophy of Education, 37*(2), 241–251. https://doi.org/10.1111/1467-9752.00323

Palmer, P. J. (1998). *The courage to teach: Exploring the inner landscape of a teacher's life.* Jossey-Bass.

Ronfeldt, M., Farmer, S. O., McQueen, K., & Grissom, J. A. (2015). Teacher collaboration in instructional teams and student achievement. *American Educational Research Journal, 52*(3), 475–514. https://doi.org/10.3102/0002831215585562

Schön, D. A. (1983). *The reflective practitioner: How professionals think in action.* Basic Books.

Shepherd, M. (2006). Using a learning journal to improve professional practice: A journey of personal and professional self-discovery. *Reflective Practice, 7*(3), 333–348. https://doi.org/10.1080/14623940600837517

Shulman, L. S. (1998). Theory, practice, and the education of professionals. *The Elementary School Journal, 98*(5), 511–526. https://doi.org/10.1086/461912

Sizer, T. R., & Sizer, N. F. (1999). *The students are watching: Schools and the moral contract.* Beacon Press.

Soini, T., Pyhältö, K., & Pietarinen, J. (2010). Pedagogical well-being: Reflecting learning and well-being in teachers' work. *Teachers and Teaching, 16*(6), 735–751. https://doi.org/10.1080/13540602.2010.517690

Swanson, K. W., & Caskey, M. M. (2022). Mentoring dialogue and practice: A transformative experience. *Journal of Transformative Learning, 9*(1), 8–17.

Swanson, K. W., & Caskey, M. M. (2024). Community of practice: Mentoring to retain middle school teachers. *Current Issues in Middle Level Education, 28*(1), 1–12. https://doi.org/10.20429/cimle.2024.280104

Tantillo Philibert, C., Soto, C., & Veon, L. (2020). *Everyday self-care for educators: Tools and strategies for well-being.* Routledge.

van Manen, M. (1997). *Researching lived experience: Human science for an action sensitive pedagogy.* The Althouse Press.

van Manen, M. (2007). Phenomenology of practice. *Phenomenology & Practice, 1*(1), 11–30. https://doi.org/10.29173/pandpr19803

Weller Swanson, K., & Caskey, M. M. (2021). A kaleidoscopic view of mentoring dialogue and practice. *The Chronicle of Mentoring & Coaching, 5*(14), 608–613.

Wenger, E. (1998). *Communities of practice: Learning, meaning and identity.* Cambridge University Press. https://doi.org/10.1017/cbo9780511803932

Part 2

Exploring

5

Resilience, Transformative Learning, and Teacher Identity

Trekking is about forging a new path. It is about choosing a destination that does not have a well-worn trail; it is about covering new ground. It is about the challenges and promises of a new view or accomplishment. When we choose to trek, we knowingly expect the unexpected. This is why teacher-friends are so valuable—when the dilemma happens, it is good to have help and duct tape.

The purpose of this chapter is to acknowledge the challenges that are systemic (large class size, multiple meetings), socially embedded (teachers have the summer off, parenting issues), and financially constrained (low pay, frozen pay raises). We present frameworks we find valuable to our well-being: building resilience, strategizing disorienting dilemmas, and honoring a multifaceted identity. These frameworks acknowledge the complexity of how we see ourselves personally and professionally. Subsequently, we provide some light, hope, and strategies that engage deeply at the level of teacher identity.

Teaching has certain challenges that resurface year after year and that many times are out of our control. For example, universal challenges include inadequate salaries, perceived lack of respect, limited career development opportunities, and excessive workloads. Several reasons teachers leave the profession entirely include high workloads, lack of autonomy, and low job satisfaction (Booth et al., 2021). Thus, teachers are experiencing professional burnout, which includes physical, emotional, psychological, and spiritual exhaustion (Skovholt & Trotter-Mathison, 2016). Approximately 25% of teachers burn out in their first year (Fitchett et al., 2018).

In this chapter, we prompt teachers to pause, examine, and unpack the challenges they encounter (*disorienting dilemmas*) and the *assumptions* used to think and solve those challenges. Working and trekking together, teacher-friends explore positive and productive ways to respond and simultaneously reignite the joy in their teaching practice. It comes down to building resiliency, which is the ability and choice to bounce back and grow through challenges.

Resilience

Teacher resilience and well-being have been used many times as synonyms. However, in a review of research, Hascher et al. (2021) found that teacher resilience is considered the capacity to maintain and restore teacher well-being (see section on Well-being in Chapter 4). Whereas Deci and Ryan (2008) defined well-being as the result of having a positive perception of one's quality of life. Therefore, we embraced the idea that resilience is a practice, and well-being is the by-product. For example, teachers intentionally address the negative issues at school toward a positive or workable solution. Specifically, teacher well-being and resilience have outcomes that include teaching quality, teacher self-efficacy, commitment, and job satisfaction (Schleicher, 2018). Overall, a sense of teacher well-being is that there are more positive experiences than negative.

Resiliency is a process, a complex process, which develops through exposure to difficult and challenging situations. Teacher resiliency specifically is the capacity to learn to adapt and use strategies to overcome adversity and achieve "good outcomes despite serious threats to adaptation or development" (Masten, 2001, p. 228). The results of being resilient include professional commitment, job satisfaction, engagement, and well-being (Cook et al., 2017). One of the best aspects of teaching is that no two days are the same; to manage a high degree of change requires a high degree of resilience. We view resilience as a muscle, a skill, and a practice. Resilience builds muscle memory. Learning to be more resilient can also support mental health and job satisfaction.

Four Dimensions of Resilience
Mansfield et al. (2016) identified four dimensions (or factors) of resilience: professional, social, motivational, and emotional. Each dimension encompasses

skills or attitudes that provide teachers with a way to cope and move forward when a dilemma or adversity arises.

Professional factors are those that directly affect teachers at school and in the classroom. Most often, teacher education programs introduce these skills to candidates during their preparation. These skills are foundational to the teaching profession and practiced daily. Arguably, these may be the easiest to hone because they are continually being reinforced in school settings such as grade-level professional learning communities, middle school team meetings, and general professional development. Professional factors include:

- committed students,
- organization and preparation,
- effective teaching skills,
- adaptability, and
- reflection.

The goal is to strengthen our practice, both pedagogically and organizationally, resulting in our ability to be flexible when we meet unexpected challenges.

Social factors include working with students, teachers, administrators, and parents. Teaching today is typically a collaborative endeavor with professional learning communities, teams (e.g., grade level), to organize content and pedagogy for subject areas. Professional learning communities can serve as powerful organizational structures when teachers actively participate. Nevertheless, any interpersonal, collaborative structure requires patience, listening skills, and self-control. Social factors that support resilience in schools are:

- strong interpersonal and communication skills,
- problem-solving,
- developing support and relationships, and
- seeking help.

It is important to note that the desire to develop relationships and ask for help requires humility, openness for dialogue, and practice (Chapters 3 and 4). Choosing and developing teacher-friend relationships is one example of a positive social factor.

Building a resilient teaching practice also includes *motivational factors*. These are practices that keep us grounded and support the processing of a dilemma. According to Mansfield et al. (2016), the following attributes are important and useful for building resilience and being resilient. Motivational factors include:

- optimism, persistence,
- focus on improvement,
- self-efficacy, setting realistic goals and expectations,
- maintaining motivation and enthusiasm, and
- enjoying challenges.

Motivational factors can be present in the mind when a dilemma begins. We can choose which factor(s) are the most useful and significant to solve the dilemma. Lastly, we must determine the goal we want to achieve. It is important to understand that motivation, organization, and optimism do not keep troubles and frustrations at bay, but they are vital for faster processing and possibly fewer consequences.

The conversations we have with ourselves are an important element of our professional processing. *Emotional factors* are those that affect our inner dialogue. It is impossible not to have an emotional response to a difficult parent meeting, an administrative decision that does not make sense to us, or a change in our teaching assignment. Emotional factors are habits that help us control our reactions, manage how intensely we respond, and how quickly we can return to a place of well-being. Emotional factors include:

- sense of humor,
- not taking things personally,
- regulating emotion,
- bouncing back from challenges,
- coping skills, and
- caring for one's own well-being.

Emotional growth is a practice that is important in a teacher's professional longevity. It provides balance to the demands of students and colleagues. It shapes our view of success and shortcomings. It is also foundational for building and sustaining a long-term professional career that is satisfying, challenging, and that grows our capacity. Teaching requires a strong but flexible disposition. Resilience can play out on a spectrum depending on the situation. It uses many different skills and elicits many different feelings.

Resilience is developmental and is a lifelong pursuit (Luthar & Brown, 2007). According to Luthar and Brown (2007), "the presence of support, love, and security fosters resilience in part, by reinforcing people's innate strengths (such as self-efficacy, positive emotions, and emotion regulation)…" (p. 947). For teachers, resilience is more than the capacity to survive and thrive in adversity. It encompasses the capacity to function well in a teaching and learning environment, including in moments of adversity that disrupt the normal flow.

> *The nature and sustainability of resilience in teachers over the course of their professional lives is not a static or innate state, but influenced, individually and in combination, by the strength of their vocational selves, the commitment of those whom they meet as part of their daily work and the quality of leadership support within the school as well as their capacities to manage anticipated and unanticipated personal events.*
>
> (Luthar & Brown, 2007, p. 947)

In other words, resilience continues to develop over a teachers' career span. As noted, teacher resiliency and well-being are often among the findings from research about the teacher retention crisis. Thus, it is helpful to better understand what encourages mid-career teachers to stay in the profession and to build their capacity to adapt to current educational challenges.

Hydration Station: Teacher Well-being and Resiliency

We offer some key ideas gleaned from recent scholars and researchers. Their ideas may align with your own ideas about how to maintain your well-being and resilience in today's climate.

- "Complexity is about getting our heads around what is possible (because anything could happen) rather than what is probably going to happen (which is determined by what has happened before)" (Berger, 2015 & Johnston, p. 11).
- Teachers who initiate advancing their skills and improving their cultures demonstrate resilience, possibly modeling it (Patterson et al., 2004).
- Around 75% or more of resilient teachers identified supportive relationships with their colleagues as a positive critical influence on their capacity to maintain their original vocation or call to teach (Day & Gu, 2010).
- Veteran teachers stated reasons for staying include purpose in teaching, positive relationships, passion for teaching, supportive school culture, passion for curricular content, accommodating work schedule, and no other opportunities available (Mullen et al., 2021).

- "Teachers who develop higher levels of resilience feel less emotionally drained, derive a greater sense of satisfaction from their work, and can interact positively with others" (Richards et al., 2016, p. 530).
- When teachers are resilient, the direct outcomes are "job satisfaction, commitment, efficacy, motivation, well-being and positive sense of identity" (Mansfield & Beltman, 2019, p. 583).

Understanding our ability to build resilience empowers how we live at school and at home. It is good to know that striving on our own is not the most effective strategy, so working together with a trusted teacher-friend is ideal. An essential part of being resilient is understanding the process of working through a disorienting dilemma. In the next section, we discuss the parts and process of a disorienting dilemma that catches us by surprise, or we find overwhelming. What separates a problem from a dilemma is that to resolve a dilemma requires an examination of our assumptions that, in the end, deeply impacts how we view ourselves and the world.

Journal Prompt: Resilence

When we are resilient and test our endurance, we can see and acknowledge our strength and the ability to persevere. The following journal prompts focus on those times when you could tangibly see your personal struggles or growth.

Write or discuss how you might exhibit resilience in the following five areas:

- Emotional regulation: The ability to manage emotions effectively
- Optimism: Maintaining a positive outlook toward future possibilities
- Problem-solving skills: The capability to analyze situations and devise practical solutions
- Social support: The readiness to seek help and support from others
- Self-efficacy: A strong belief in one's ability to meet challenges

Transformative Learning

Resiliency that empowers teachers over an entire career implies that teachers grow and transform as they learn, experience positive and negative challenges and build enduring skills. Transformation is the process in which we "learn to negotiate and act on our own purposes, values, feelings and meanings rather than those we have uncritically assimilated from others—to gain greater control over our lives a socially responsible, clear-thinking decisions makers" (Mezirow, 2000, p. 8). In this section, we discuss the steps of disorienting dilemmas. This process requires dialogue and practice, grappling with assumptions, and a willingness to expand.

As adults, we learn through experiences every day. Sometimes it is fun to see how far we have come. Our lived experience hones our values, feelings, and frames of reference. These experiences shape and respond to our assumptions.

Karen: Transformative Learning

I have come from a long line of teachers. I even had my mother as a teacher in high school. I had an assumption that I was born to be a teacher. This assumption shaped my college years, my career choice, and my high level of job satisfaction. However, when the opportunity arose to become a professor, I had to unpack, sort out, and repack many assumptions. I reimagined what it meant to be a teacher, as a dyslexic, I challenged held assumptions that I was a bad writer, as a wife, I even had to reorganize my role in marriage. In other words, an opportunity presented itself, but to move forward, I had to "rearrange the furniture" in my mind and work through assumptions that could have kept me from seriously considering getting a doctorate. Did I do all this rearranging on my own? No.

Micki: Transformative Learning

I loved being a teacher of inner-city youth. I held the assumption that this was my true calling and that I would never leave classroom teaching to pursue an administrative credential or seek another career. I firmly believed my place was in the classroom and where I could make a difference. So, when another school offered me a position as a curriculum integration specialist, I hesitated—much to the dismay of the principal. This was not in my world view nor what I planned for myself, so I needed time to grapple with the idea of leaving the classroom. After much soul searching and heart-felt conversation with my husband, I took the leap. Thus, I had to reevaluate my assumptions about myself as a classroom teachers and deal with the discomfort of making a life-changing decision.

The process of re-evaluating or reflection requires a critical friend and the assessment of assumptions. It is through conversation that we find our voice and question how we define ourselves. Many times, the opportunity to grow comes through a struggle or problem that we cannot solve with our current set of skills. This is a disorienting dilemma.

Disorienting Dilemmas

Understanding a disorienting dilemma can foster new frames of reference that are necessary to lead healthier, more effective, and fulfilling lives. A dilemma can be big or small. It can be continuously annoying like a difficult parent at school or a significant moment in life such as a death. Mezirow (2000) referred to the result of working through a disorienting dilemma as transformative learning; the possibilities of approaching a dilemma with the goal to question ourselves, stretch intellectually, and be fundamentally changed by the process. The idea goes beyond how to individually work through difficult situations but rather focuses on how or when we approach dilemmas through a lens of change, personal growth.

Transformative learning refers to the process by which we transform our taken-for-granted frames of reference (meaning perspectives, habits of mind, and mindsets) to become more inclusive, discriminating, open, emotionally capable of change, and reflective so that they may generate beliefs and opinions that prove more true and justified to guide action (Mezirow, 2000, pp. 7–8).

As described by Mezirow (1981), a disorienting dilemma is the moment when the individual "becomes critically conscious of how and why our habits of perception, thought and action have distorted the way we have defined the problem and ourselves in relationship to it" (p. 65). In short, our current ways of thinking about a problem no longer work. A dilemma is a threat and therefore sparks the pursuit of problem-solving. The skill set and frame of mind that we would normally use to solve a problem are no longer sufficient for the task at hand. The reason a disorienting dilemma is transformative is that it requires an examination of the assumptions we bring to the problem; this is deep work and many times requires the support of a critical friend to ask us the hard questions. Transformative learning from a disorienting dilemma often follows some variation of these nine phases:

1. *Self-examination with feelings of fear, anger, guilt, or shame.* What are we facing that is so challenging that we are stopped from moving forward? Is there a way to get to the heart of the resistance in our minds to find space for a new approach?
2. *A critical assessment of assumptions.* Are there patterns of evaluating and problem-solving that do not reflect our new roles in life, new challenges? What are those assumptions, and which are we willing to abandon for newer crafted frameworks?
3. *Recognition that one's discontent and the process of transformation are paired.* One key sign that a dilemma is about to challenge us deeply is a grand sense of dissatisfaction. Every strategy we try falls short or does not fit. The only way to find satisfaction is to bravely go

through the process of unpacking, re-evaluating, and repacking. Beware that this can be a costly process in which friends, colleagues, and family become unhappy with the new you. It can be costly to hold a changing view of work, faith, and your identity. What we held true previously may no longer be true.

4. *An exploration of options for new roles, relationships, and actions.* Because the shift in your thinking has been foundational, the search for alternatives to past roles and relationships is necessary. These roles may be the ones we play in our families of origin, our immediate families, our roles as teachers, our roles in collaborative groups, our friendship circles, and in how we define our boundaries.

5. *Planning a new course of action.* It is reasonable that if we are asking ourselves hard questions, taking new action would soon follow. Remember that the disorienting dilemma came about due to dissatisfaction in the first place. This does not mean quitting your job and starting over. However, it does imply permission to explore and consider big and small changes to your current life.

6. *Acquiring knowledge and skills for implementing one's plans.* The exploration can be the fun part. Have you been toying with becoming an administrator? What does that mean? Where do you get that certification? What is the cost? Why is the cost/benefit analysis?

7. *Provisional trying of new roles.* You are transforming, the old roles are less comfortable, and the new roles are not yet known. So, what can you try without making a solid commitment? Can you shadow a colleague who is an administrator, counselor, or entrepreneur? Can you be the teacher who leaves on time and doesn't take work home?

8. *Building competence and self-confidence in new roles and relationships.* Starting to build new practices through dialogue with our teacher-friends who support our growth can provide us with the support needed to make changes. As new ideas are tried and tested, they build our confidence, and we meet new people along the way and as a result resolve the pending dilemma.

9. *A reintegration into one's life based on conditions dictated by one's new perspective.* The result is that transformation has happened as a result of the hard work. We see work, home, and life differently and cannot go back to seeing it the way we did prior to the dilemma.

Choosing to do the hard work of examining our assumptions, asking for critical feedback from a teacher-friend, and trying new roles and approaches takes courage, persistence, and patience. The outcome, however, is to lead a more fulfilling and happier life. In line with our trekking metaphor, transformation is a process of discovery. It is embarking on a trek that has an unknown destination therefore the journey must be the goal.

The next section discusses how as adults we have multiple identities. Adulting is complex, dynamic, and fascinating. Our roles, expectations, and dreams change with new information, opportunities, and challenges. Who we are is not singular—but multifaceted.

Teacher Identity

We have referred to a teacher identity in previous chapters. All humans hold multiple identities such as spouse, parent, child, teacher, leader, and partner. In the teacher-friend mentoring approach, we acknowledge that personal and professional life overlap and inform each other. Our identity shifts and shapes as it is influenced by our experiences. According to Sachs (2005):

> *Teacher professional identity then stands at the core of the teaching profession. It provides a framework for teachers to construct their own ideas of "how to be," "how to act" and "how to understand" their work and their place in society. Importantly, teacher identity is not something that is fixed nor is it imposed; rather it is negotiated through experience and the sense that is made of that experience.*
>
> (p. 15)

Delving further into the literature, we find other scholars' thoughts about teacher identity. For example, Wenger (1998) makes a clear link between the personal and professional self of a teacher. They are "mirror images of one another" and the same five characteristics apply to both: identity is the negotiated experience of self, involves community membership, has a learning trajectory, combines different forms of membership within an identity, and presumes involvement in local and global contexts (p. 149). His position links identity very closely with practice.

Others connect teacher identity to teacher agency. For instance, Day et al. (2006) suggest the importance of understanding that a teacher's identity has multiple dimensions, some stable and some unstable. He posits that teacher agency may be involved in the maintenance or further shaping of multiple identities and the attention to tensions among them. Similarly, Parkison (2008) contends that identity plays a crucial role in the ways teachers perform within institutions and society. Their sense of agency, facilitated by their identities, can be a powerful force for good.

In our own experience, we think of identity as a bag of trail mix. We are both:

- mothers, daughters, wives, and sisters
- scholars, researchers, and authors
- friends, colleagues, and acquaintances
- happy, sad, joyful, and disappointed
- energetic and tired
- extroverted and introverted

Teachers' multiple identities are active, interrelated, and inextricably woven together. This is important in the discussion about resilience and dilemmas because it is easy to view ourselves singularly as a teacher at work and a parent and spouse at home. However, every part of our identity influences others. Many teachers parent students in their classes. Many parents are teachers at home. According to Hammerness et al. (2005):

> *Developing an identity as a teacher is an important part of securing teachers' commitment to their work and adherence to professional norms ... the identities teachers develop shape their dispositions, where they place their effort, whether and how they seek out professional development opportunities, and what obligations they see as intrinsic to their role.*
>
> (pp. 383–384)

We concur and see value in embracing how identity informs our practice. We also believe that teacher-friends can remind us when teaching or life becomes difficult and that approaching a challenge is easier if we bring our whole being into the problem-solving process. Likewise, when trekking and the trail is flat, lunch was good, and the view is beautiful that the gratitude we experience informs our whole.

Conclusion

In this chapter we have covered a lot of ground. It was important for us to acknowledge that teaching is hard and so closely tied to our hearts. We began with well-being and resilience because these concepts are tightly connected and keep teachers in the profession.

Resiliency is muscle memory that supports well-being. Reflective practice is key and innate to teaching. We plan on our way to work in the morning and review how those plans went on the drive home. But there are times when there is a feeling that cannot be shaken, a deeper notion that new skills or frameworks are ready to be explored. The use of reflection as transformative learning is hard work, but essential to grow personally and professionally. It is essential to understand the elements of our teacher's identity so we can identify what areas influence us as teachers and manage them.

The purpose of this book is to acknowledge the role that teacher-friends play in our individual growth. Supportive collegial relationships are essential for developing and sustaining teacher resilience (Mansfield et al., 2016). As asserted by Kegan (1994), the two greatest human yearnings are to be included and to have agency. We love this! As teachers, we want to be part of a dynamic profession and to make decisions that positively advance our goals. Summarizing these thoughts, Hascher et al. (2021) offered:

> *We need to better understand how to enhance teacher wellbeing as a driving source for personal and professional flourishing. Ultimately, this will contribute to the profession as a whole because it can lead to an empowering of teachers to care for their students, create positive learning environments, commit to the role of education, and support a learning society.*
>
> (p. 429)

In other words, attending to your well-being as teachers is paramount for your personal and professional growth.

Trail Talk

We suggest that teacher-friends often share their expertise and learn from one another. This reciprocal exchange is an investment in each other and improves your professional lives. During this exchange, you may discuss and unpack a disorienting dilemma (e.g., an incident or situation) that challenged your assumptions or was a point of confusion. Talking through the dilemma might have led to a shift—a transformation.

- ◆ Do you feel more comfortable sharing your expertise or listening to someone else's?
- ◆ How does talking through a disorienting dilemma help you process it?
- ◆ What do you think helps you to be resilient?
- ◆ What recent learning experience did you find to be transformative?

References

Berger, J., & Johnston, K. (2015). *Simple habits for complex times: Powerful practices for leaders.* Stanford Business Press.

Booth, J., Coldwell, M., Müller, L.-M., Perry, E., & Zuccollo, J. (2021). Mid-career teachers: A mixed methods scoping study of professional development, career progression and retention. *Education Sciences, 11*(6), 299. https://doi.org/10.3390/educsci11060299

Cook, C. R., Miller, F. G., Fiat, A., Renshaw, T. L., Frye, M., Joseph, G., & Decano, P. (2017). Promoting secondary teacher's well-being and intentions to implement evidence-based practices: Randomized evaluation of the achiever resilience curriculum. *Psychology in the Schools, 54*(1), 13–28. https://doi.org/10.1002/pits.21980

Day, C., & Gu, Q. (2010). *The new lives of teachers.* Routledge.

Day, C., Kington, A., Stobart, G., & Sammons, P. (2006). The personal and professional selves of teachers: Stable and unstable identities. *British Educational Research Journal, 32*(4), 601–616.

Deci, E. L., & Ryan, R. M. (2008). Self-determination theory: A macrotheory of human motivation, development, and health. *Canadian Psychology, 49*(3), 182–185. https://doi.org/10.1037/a0012801

Fitchett, P. G., McCarthy, C. J., Lambert, R. G., & Boyle, L. (2018). An examination of US first-year teachers' risk for occupational stress: Associations with professional preparation and occupational health. *Teachers and Teaching, 24*(2), 99–118. https://doi.org/10.1080/13540602.2017.1386648

Hammerness, K., Darling-Hammond, L., & Bransford, J. (2005). How teachers learn and develop. In L. Darling-Hammond, & J. Bransford (Eds.), *Preparing teachers for a changing world: What teachers should learn and be able to do* (pp. 358–389). Jossey-Bass.

Hascher, T., Beltman, S., & Mansfield, C. (2021). Teacher wellbeing and resilience: Towards an integrative model. *Educational Research, 63*(4), 416–439. https://doi.org/10.1080/00131881.2021.1980416

Kegan, R. (1994). *In over our heads. The mental demands of modern life.* Harvard University Press.

Luthar, S. S., & Brown, P. J. (2007). Maximizing resilience through diverse levels of inquiry: Prevailing paradigms, possibilities, and priorities for the future. *Development and Psychopathology, 19*(3), 931–955. https://doi.org/10.1017/S0954579407000454

Mansfield, C., & Beltman, S. (2019). Promoting resilience for teachers: Pre-service and in-service professional learning. *The Australian Educational Researcher, 46*(4), 583–588. https://doi.org/10.1007/s13384-019-00347-x

Mansfield, C. F., Beltman, S., Broadley, T., & Weatherby-Fell, N. (2016). Building resilience in teacher education: An evidenced informed framework. *Teaching and Teacher Education, 54*, 77–87. https://doi.org/10.1016/j.tate.2015.11.016

Masten, A. S. (2001). Ordinary magic: Resilience processes in development. *The American Psychologist, 56*(3), 227–238. https://doi.org/10.1037//0003-066X.56.3.227

Mezirow, J. (1981). A critical theory of adult learning and education. *Adult Education Quarterly, 32*(1), 3–24. https://doi.org/10.1177/074171368103200101

Mezirow, J. (2000). *Learning as transformation. Critical perspectives on a theory in progress.* Jossey Bass.

Mullen, C. A., Tienken, C. H., & Shields, L. (2021). Developing teacher resilience and resilient school cultures. *AASA Journal of Scholarship and Practice, 18*(1), 8–24.

Parkison, P. (2008). Space for performing teacher identity: Through the lens of Kafka and Hegel. *Teachers and Teaching: Theory and Practice, 14*(1), 51–60. https://doi.org/10.1080/13540600701837640

Patterson, J. H., Collins, L., & Abbot, G. (2004). A study of teacher resilience in urban schools. *Journal of Instructional Psychology, 31*(1), 3–11.

Richards, K. A. R., Levesque-Bristol, C., Templin, T. J., & Graber, K. C. (2016). The impact of resilience on role stressors and burnout in elementary and secondary teachers. *Social Psychology of Education, 19*(3), 511–536. https://psycnet.apa.org/doi/10.1007/s11218-016-9346-x

Sachs, J. (2005). Teacher education and the development of professional identity: Learning to be a teacher. In P. Denicolo, & M. Kompf (Eds.), *Connecting policy and practice: Challenges for teaching and learning in schools and universities* (pp. 5–21). Routledge.

Schleicher, A. (2018). *Valuing our teachers and raising their status: How communities can help.* International Summit on the Teaching Profession, OECD Publishing. https://doi.org/10.1787/9789264292697-en

Skovholt, T. M., & Trotter-Mathison, M. (2016). *The resilient practitioner: Burnout and compassion fatigue prevention and self-care strategies for the helping professions* (3rd ed.). Routledge.

Wenger, E. (1998). *Communities of practice.* Cambridge University Press. https://doi.org/10.1017/cbo9780511803932

6
Packing, Unpacking, and Repacking

This chapter is a favorite of ours because we believe educators want to reach into the heart of their practice. In learning more, we also learn that we do not know many things. This understanding provides an opportunity to be creative, invoke imagination, put off assumptions, and bring order to chaos.

When we read Joan Wink's book (2011) *Critical Pedagogy: Notes from the Real World*, her idea of learning, unlearning, and relearning resonated with us at both personal and professional levels. Though learning has been a motivating factor for us, Wink's work energized us. As we delved into Wink's work on challenging assumptions about teaching and replacing those long-held assumptions with new information and ideas, we found ourselves more open to accepting this challenge.

To hold to the trekking theme of teacher-friend mentoring, we are adapting Wink's (2011) notion of learning, unlearning, and relearning to packing, unpacking, and repacking our backpacks. In other words, we come into the work of teaching with preparation, college degrees, having been students ourselves, and hopes for ourselves and our students. We bring so much of ourselves into the experience of teaching—trekking to familiar places and new destinations—that we may need to examine what we have packed for the trip, unpack some items that no longer serve their purpose, and repack after doing research on what is new and available.

Reflective Practice: Talking and Writing to Learn

Reflective and reflexive practice differs from the more commonly known reflective practice. In reflective practice, the intention is to thoughtfully review what has happened. According to Bolton (2009), reflection is "a state of mind, an ongoing constituent of practice. [It] can enable practitioners to learn from experience about themselves, their work and the way they relate to home and work, significant others and wider society and cultures" (p. 752). We acknowledge that a required reflection may only hit the surface of our practice. On the contrary, reflexivity is an internal dialogue that can lead to action and transform practice (Archer, 2012). Thus, we challenge you to consider more deeply the context of teaching, the power embedded in schools, and the possibility of not having answers to many of today's questions.

As Bolton (2009) highlights, reflection and reflexivity touch on three areas:

- Personal and professional identities, actions, and reactions are our individual responsibility
- Identify and voice where there is an imbalance of power and diversity
- Being open to questions, not finding answers, and doubt

Reflexivity walks alongside reflection in that it requires looking for ways or strategies to question our assumptions, habits, and thought processes as we consider the complexity of how we fit into a larger context of others. To this end, we find it most powerful to reflect alongside others—our teacher-friends. Taken together, reflection and reflexivity are more difficult to do alone or in isolation. Trekking is also harder to do alone; there are many decisions to make, observations to be shared, and support to be found when trekking with a partner.

So, where do teacher-friends begin to reflect on their personal and professional experiences? It may be helpful to return to the trekking metaphor. When designing a trek, the destination may or may not be specific. This is not to imply an ill-fated trip but to open to wandering. A common phrase today is, "not all who wander are lost." This holds true for reflective practice. While the destination may be to examine staying in the teaching profession, the list of considerations and processes to learn more about them can be elusive. We argue that it is time to start the journey and discover new possibilities along the way and to put down held assumptions that limit our perspectives.

Reflection is a way to examine what happened in a situation, what that situation may have looked like or how it may have been perceived by others involved, being willing to ask questions about it and scrutinize our assumptions and to apply outside information to inform our thinking about the situation.

Karen: Talking and Writing as Reflection

In conducting research for this chapter, I came across an idea that strongly suggests we have the most to learn from what we do not remember or do not consider important. This seems odd but makes sense to me when I think about all the junk at the bottom of my backpack. For example, when unpacking, I find a granola bar wrapper that I do not remember eating, a safety pin that I don't remember packing, and a charger that does not even work on my phone. I could simply put them all in the garbage or take time to consider why or how they ended up on the trip and in my pack.

In my teaching practice, there is a similar unpacking that is required. A simple example would be seating charts. I make and remake seating charts at least every unit or quarter. This is a long-held practice. However, when I unpack it philosophically, is it still a practice that I find useful, necessary, biased, or no longer necessary? What do seating charts mean to students? What happens if I let students sit where they want? What is the impact on their attention, self-esteem, and performance? Are seating charts primarily a control mechanism for me as a teacher, or am I providing students an opportunity to learn from new students other than their friends? The short answer is yes to all the possibilities. More unpacking is needed.

One approach to reflective practice is storytelling. When I eat lunch with my teacher-friends, it is always a storytelling session about our families, students, or school. Storytelling helps us order our thoughts and feelings about an event. Learning is both a cognitive process and an emotional one. The process of telling a story requires a multitude of decisions to be made about what to tell, from what perspective to tell it, the emotions to evoke in the listener and the teller, the questions to ask ourselves or to be asked about the incident, and also the unasked or examine elements of the incident. This sounds complicated, but we find it creative, invigorating, and challenging.

Micki: Talking and Writing as Reflection

I also learn from what I intentionally pack and the untapped treasures lurking inside the many pockets of my messenger bag (aka teacher backpack). Naturally, it holds my basic materials: a laptop, sticky notes, pens and highlighters, and, most importantly, a professional journal for capturing my thoughts and noting ideas. These basic materials are readily at hand—whether at school, home, or elsewhere. I may also discover untapped treasures when I unpack my bag. These may take the form of business cards and assorted items collected at professional conferences. I can simply recycle the business cards, as I may not immediately recall why I took them. Or I can take time to think back on the interaction with a person who gave me their card and why I wanted to be in contact with them. I may also come across a pen, promotional flyers, or sample materials gathered from the exhibit hall. Why do I have these? Are they for use in my classroom, for one of my colleagues, or for my students? Of course, as a teacher, I know these untapped treasures are part of my practice. So, I need to take time to consider what to do about these treasures.

One of my decades-long practices has been to negotiate the day's curriculum with my students: middle school students, high school students, and university students. At each of these levels, I posted the agenda for the day's lesson or session. After reviewing the agenda, I would ask the students if they wanted any changes to the agenda (e.g., topics, order of topics). Why did I do this? What was the reasoning behind my decision to start every class in the same way? What did students think about my attempts to negotiate the day's lesson with them? Was I truly promoting a more democratic classroom, or was I only giving this notion lip service? In other words, how did this practice promote or suppress learning in my classroom?

My approach to reflective practice has two complementary facets: talking with a teacher-friend and writing in my professional journal. Engaging in dialogue, conversation, or good talk (Chapter 3) with a teacher-friend allows me to vocalize my thinking, concerns, and questions about my practice (e.g., curriculum negotiation). During this exchange, I also seek their open and honest questions to help me unpack a particular practice. Talking with a teacher-friend in this way helps my thinking. Similarly, writing in my journal helps my thinking. I see writing as a type of thinking. Putting words on paper helps me to clarify my ideas, uncover points of confusion, and identify some actions or next steps. While these two reflective practices are not unique, they are central to my practice and growth as a teacher.

Effective Reflective Practice

In Chapter 4, we shared our thoughts about practice: trekking, mentoring, listening, and learning. We suggested that reflecting deeply and for the purpose of learning more about our practice and assumptions was important to advance the possibilities for new ideas and experiences. Bolton and Delderfield (2018) expressed these ideas:

> *Effective reflective practice and reflexivity meet the paradoxical need both to tell and retell our stories in order for us to feel secure enough, and yet critically examine our actions, and those of others, in order to increase our understanding of ourselves and our practice and develop dynamically.*
>
> (p. 10)

In short, we have found teaching and living to be highly complex, and our decisions are embedded in political and socially constructed norms.

What to Pack, Unpack, and Repack

During the first teaching years (one to four), all teachers do is pack. We fill our backpack with curriculum content and objectives, instructional routines and strategies, and assessment techniques and manage the workload of being a novice teacher. Then, as we become mid-career teachers, we unpack what is inside our backpacks. We have the time and experience to look more closely at what we carry. As we become more fully aware of our practice, including our assumptions about teaching, we can identify more clearly our own needs as teachers. In the following passages, we explore this notion of teachers' packing, unpacking, and repacking.

What to Pack

Novice teachers pack everything possible such as:

- figuring out how to reach, teach, and manage our students;
- planning lessons to address curriculum standards and assessing student learning;
- interacting with and responding to the administrator and fellow teachers' expectations;
- learning the cultural norms of our school and community; and
- coping with the incredibly demanding workload of being a teacher.

They may bring along learnings or remnants from their teacher preparation program. They may also hold tightly to the assumptions that they have about teaching and themselves as teachers.

As mid-career teachers, you may pack the following essentials:

- teaching expertise (i.e., curriculum, instruction, assessment),
- personal and professional goals, and
- a positive mindset about your practice.

We liken these essentials to the water bottle, sunglasses, sunscreen, map, and compass that a trekker carries in their backpack. They are the basic necessities for going on a trek. Some fortunate trekkers may also bring along a journal to record their thoughts or walking sticks to ease their travel. In any case, the trekker is prepared to start their journey.

What to Unpack

Mid-career teachers begin to unpack the essentials, including the assumptions they have carried since entering the profession. These assumptions may include:

- how their students learn individually and collectively,
- what constitutes best practice, and
- their personal and professional identity.

Because mid-career teachers are no longer scrambling to prepare for each day, they can seize the space for reflection. They know how to teach, yet they want to know more. They can also become more mindful about their teaching practice and professional identity.

Regarding our identity as teachers, we value the insights of Caprar et al. (2022):

> *A more useful takeaway is the value of a reflective and mindful relationship with one's identifications. The analogy of a pair of sunglasses is instructive here: it is one thing to deliberately put them on for good reasons (e.g., protecting one's eyes, improving visibility); it is quite another to forget one is even wearing them, and needlessly see the world with filtered vision. Identities are similarly helpful when deployed thoughtfully, but, as we have shown, they can wreak havoc when adopted and enacted thoughtlessly.*
>
> (p. 789)

In other words, we may need to remove our sunglasses (i.e., perspectives) to see more clearly what brings us joy in teaching. We believe mid-career is an ideal time to set aside unrealistic expectations, lean in and listen to our teacher-friends, and illuminate possibilities through mutual mentoring.

This time of unpacking is emptying the contents of your backpack to see what is inside: what weighs you down and lifts you up. You may discover you need different items, as well as a smaller or bigger backpack, for your trekking adventure.

What to Repack

Mid-career is also the perfect time to repack. It makes sense, right? Mid-career teachers get to decide what to repack, including:

- assumptions about their teaching practice,
- expectations of and goals for themselves,
- theories and ideas to explore, and
- opportunities to seize.

Alongside these items to repack, mid-career teachers often include courage, hope, openness, and joy—all of which fuel their passion for teaching. Together, these repacked essentials help foster renewed energy for teaching, especially during turbulent times.

Repacking is like selecting tools that are better suited for the trek ahead. As an experienced trekker, you select and include items to help you go the distance, such as a waterproof map, adjustable walking sticks, a lightweight refillable water bottle, and more comfortable hiking shoes.

We believe that unpacking and repacking are key facets of mid-career teaching. Teachers at this stage are engaging in an ongoing cycle of unpacking and repacking their practice. In doing so, they are growing professionally. We believe that working side-by-side with a teacher-friend is a fabulous way to travel. Our teacher-friends, as mutual mentors, can join us in cycles of unpacking and repacking. Not only can we learn and grow alongside our teacher-friends, but we can also learn from their prior experience. When we trek together, we are engaging in individual and collective critical reflection that can produce a much more rewarding and satisfying experience.

Using Critical Reflection to Unpack Practice

As we shared in Chapter 4 (Practice), teachers can engage in critically reflective practice to explore how they work. We briefly introduced Stephen Brookfield's (1998, 2017) ideas regarding the stance that educators must continually research their own assumptions about teaching using four lenses: autobiographical, learners' eyes, colleagues' perceptions, and theoretical (see Figure 6.1).

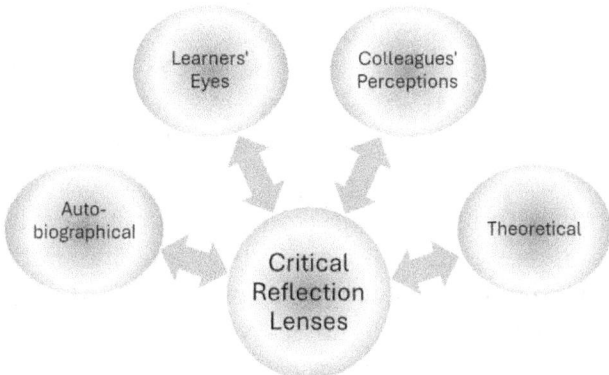

Figure 6.1 Brookfield's (2017) Lenses of Critical Reflection

Experienced teachers, like you, have been using some or all of these lenses to critically examine their practice. We use a magnifying glass as a metaphor for peering through these four lenses. In the next paragraphs, we describe and explain Brookfield's lenses of critical reflection.

Autobiographical Lens

The autobiographical lens is our *personal experience*. According to Brookfield (2017), this lens "gets the least respect" (p. 69). Why is this? Because many researchers viewed personal experience as anecdotal and too subjective. In other words, these experiences are unique and not generalizable. However, as Brookfield insists:

- "accounts of personal experiences typically move us more than summaries of findings in a research study" (p. 69).
- "Specific experiences always have universal elements embedded within them" (p. 70).
- "Personal experiences of learning are intertwined with teaching practice" (p. 70).

We agree about the power of personal experience to inform teaching practice. We bet you do too!

Certainly, you remember those "teachable moments" when you seize an opportunity to connect a real-world event to the day's lesson. You also may recall and ruminate on an incident that gave you pause while teaching. In other words, you reflect on your personal experience with teaching. Likewise, when you engage in dialogue, conversation, or good talk with a teacher-friend about your teaching successes or difficulties, you are sharing accounts of your personal experience with teaching. You are sharing stories from your practice. As you share stories, you reflect more deeply on your own personal experiences.

When you are trekking alone, you can engage in critical reflection through self-dialogue (see Chapter 3). Self-dialogue is an internal dialogue you have with yourself. You can either talk with yourself by taking on different positions or imagine talking with a thought partner (Oleś et al., 2020). This type of internal dialogue allows you to deeply consider aspects of your teaching practice. Not only does self-dialogue promote critical reflection, but it also offers you the opportunity to prepare for conversing with others (Fernyhough, 2016). In other words, you can reflect and mentally rehearse what you want to say in an upcoming conversation. Whether talking with yourself or an imagined partner, self-dialogue is a valuable tool for critical reflection about your trekking adventures in teaching.

The Learners' Eyes

Through the lens of *students' eyes* teachers can tap into how their students are experiencing learning. According to Brookfield (2017), this lens helps you explore "how students are experiencing learning so you can build bridges that take them from where they are now to a new destination" (p. 62). In other words, we learn about our teaching from our students. We put the students at the center of our teaching practice. Brookfield offers a few major points when seeking information from students.

- Ensuring anonymity when first seeking student feedback is much more likely to result in honest and accurate information. "Students who are genuinely sure that their responses are anonymous are much more likely to tell the truth" (p. 63).
- The best response to student feedback is non-defensive. Refrain from explaining or defending your practice when receiving student criticism.
- Getting student feedback takes time, yet its value outweighs the time expended. "The only way we can know if students are learning what we intend for them to learn is by checking in with them" (p. 65).

We believe that looking at practice from our students' perspective can prompt us to examine our assumptions about what they are learning.

Sometimes you can sense or literally see that students are not learning what you are teaching. You perceive a noticeable gap between your teaching and their learning. So, in the moment, you make decisions: plow through the lesson, pivot and try something new, make a mental note for later reflection, or pause and talk with the students. All are valid responses. As you might anticipate, we suggest tapping into student voice. Perhaps you already look at your teaching through students' eyes. If so, please share your ideas with your colleagues, especially a teacher-friend who has yet to seek students' perspectives. We also recommend using the *Critical Incident Questionnaire* (Brookfield, 2017) or another strategy (e.g., exit slip, Muddiest Point, midpoint check-in) to gather student feedback anonymously. Check these out in the Connections to Practice section.

Colleagues' Perceptions

Colleagues' perceptions are invaluable for examining our assumptions about teaching. As Brookfield (2017) asserted, "The presence of critical friends is at the heart of the critically reflective process" (p. 66) and insisted that the "best teaching colleagues are critical friends" (p. 66). In other words, these peers are our teacher-friends. As Brookfield reminds:

- "A critical friend is someone who strives to help you unearths and check your assumptions and opens you up to new perspectives about familiar problems" (p. 66).
- "Talking to colleagues unravels the shroud of silence in which our work is wrapped" (p. 66).
- "…when colleagues function as critical friends they affirm that our problems are not idiosyncratic blemishes that we need to keep hidden but shared dilemmas" (p. 68).

We agree wholeheartedly with Brookfield's thoughts about interacting with critical friends to learn about ourselves as teachers. We view a critical friend as our teacher-friend—a colleague who serves as a mirror for us to see ourselves more completely.

Given your years of teaching experience, you may already have a teacher-friend that you seek out about your practice. You can communicate openly by using dialogue, conversation, or good talk with this teacher-friend (Chapter 3). Not only can this teacher-friend critically reflect with you about your practice, but they can also serve as a trekking partner when exploring uncharted ground. Consider some of these ideas. You can decide to participate in the same professional development workshop and talk about its practical value during your planning period. Similarly, you can select the same book to read and talk about its relevance over lunch. For example, you may want to learn more about anxious students, so you pick up Hannah Beach and Tamara Neufeld Strijack's (2020) book, *Reclaiming Our Students: Why Children Are More Anxious, Aggressive, and Shut Down Than Ever—And What We Can Do About It*. Then you can discuss how these ideas may influence or not influence your teaching. Whatever idea you pursue, we recommend reserving time in your school day for engaging in the invaluable experience of seeing your practice through a teacher-friend's eyes.

The Theoretical Lens
Using the critical reflection lens of *theory* "is the hardest to sell" (Brookfield, 2017, p. 72). Teachers often share that they rarely have time in their busy school days to read or even think about theory. Nevertheless, Brookfield argues:

- "…sometimes reading theory can feel like coming home. You stumble upon a piece of work that puts into cogent words something you've felt but been unable to articulate" (p. 73).

- "Finding a theorist who makes explicit something you've been sensing or who states publicly what you've suspected privately but felt unable to express is wonderfully affirming" (p. 73).
- "Theory that explodes settled worldviews is important because it combats the groupthink that sometimes emerges in collegial reflection groups" (p. 74).

In other words, theoretical and philosophical or research literature can affirm or put into words what you are experiencing as a teacher.

Critically reflecting on your assumptions through a theoretical lens requires intentionality. We think delving into articles or books can satisfy curiosities, introduce new ideas, or disrupt long-held beliefs. The best part is you get to choose what theory, philosophy, or research to consider and use as a reflective lens. One idea is to read the book that everyone at your school or in your community seems to be talking about. For instance, you may opt to read Gholdy Muhammad's (2023) newest book, *Unearthing Joy: A Guide to Culturally and Historically Responsive Curriculum and Instruction*. Her focus on joy may capture your attention and may call to mind the ways you find joy in your teaching. Another idea is to pick a controversial book or article to read that disrupts your thinking and moves you toward an alternate path. Again, we encourage you to make time during your school day (e.g., 20 minutes of silent sustained reading) to consider ideas from the literature that relate to your practice. We believe this time for professional reading is well spent.

Hydration Station: Reflection

As mid-career teachers, you have experience reflecting on your own practice. Nevertheless, you may wish to consider what others say about reflection, reflexivity, critical reflection, and assumptions about teaching. You may share common ground with or find validation in the following points.

- "Reflection involves taking the unprocessed, raw material of experience and engaging with it as a way to make sense of what has occurred" (Boud, 2001).
- "Reflection becomes reflexivity when informed and intentional internal dialogue leads to changes in educational practices, expectations, and beliefs. Reflexivity can promote deep professional learning and bring sustainable change in education" (Feucht et al., 2017, p. 234).
- Critical reflection requires an "examination of personal and professional belief systems, as well as the deliberate consideration of the ethical implications and effect of practices" (Brown, 2004, p. 91).

- ◆ Critical reflection is a key dimension of transformative learning (Mezirow, 2009).
- ◆ "Critical reflection … creates space and opportunity for individuals to understand their way of making meaning of the complex realities in the world" (Wu & Crocco, 2019, p. 409).
- ◆ All reflection is not necessarily critical reflection by nature (Brookfield, 2017).
- ◆ Collegial dialogue can help teachers see familiar issues through a new lens, challenge underlying assumptions, and gain a more holistic understanding (Sprott, 2019).
- ◆ "…we are all vulnerable to the assumption that teachers always know what to do attributing teachers' actions to their content knowledge or their character traits rather than to the situations they face" (Kennedy, 2019, p. 141).

Next, we look at ways to connect packing, unpacking, and repacking to practice.

Engaging in Practice

To tap student voice anonymously and view your practice through their eyes, we suggest using Brookfield's *Critical Incident Questionnaire* (CIQ), exit slips, plus/delta chart, and midterm letter. While all of these take time, you can learn a great deal from your students using any one of these.

CIQ (Brookfield, 1998). As experienced teachers, you may wish to seek input from your students. At the end of a week or unit, maybe a challenging week or a new unit, have your students complete a CIQ. Perhaps, you can have them complete and submit it digitally, so you get a copy and students retain a copy. After you review the CIQs, share what you learned in general with your students.

Exit Slips. As you know, teachers use exit slips to quickly gather informal input from their students at the end of class. They prompt students to complete exit slips for many purposes. For instance, you may want to know if students grasped key concepts or have questions about a topic. Similarly, you can ask students to express their feelings or opinions about a particular learning activity or instructional practice.

Plus/Delta Chart. After a lesson, at the midpoint, or at the end of the term, you can ask students to complete a plus/delta chart. Basically, this is a T-chart. On the plus side, the student lists "What worked well." On the delta side, the student lists "what needs to be changed." After collecting the plus/delta charts, read the students' responses, looking for common themes. You may wish to share what you learned with your students.

Midterm Letter. At the midpoint of a term, ask students to write you a letter expressing what they are learning in your class and what they want to learn in your class. After reading the midterm letters, summarize what you learned from your students. You may wish to write a letter to the class in response.

Conclusion

As mid-career teachers, you recognize that you carry backpacks filled with years of education, teaching experience, and life experience. Every day, you bring your many talents to students in your classroom and peers in your school. To serve your students well, you add more to your backpack. You routinely interact with school administrators, counselors, and other school personnel. You also communicate with parents and caregivers. In other words, as you well know, you have a very full backpack.

Throughout this chapter, we invited you to look inside your backpack—your practice. After describing reflective and reflexive practice, we explored packing, unpacking, and repacking your practice. Then, we took a deep dive into Brookfield's (1998) lenses of critical reflection, which can serve as a means of critically reflecting on our teaching assumptions. Ideally, this exploration helped you reflect on what you carry, what you want to keep, and what you want to set aside. Whether you added more weight or lightened your load, we wanted you to discover or rediscover what brings you joy. Perhaps you found a pathway allowing you to walk alongside a teacher-friend in a mutually beneficial trek. Or perhaps you found it beneficial to take a solo trek. What we suggested was most important was to keep trekking to both familiar places and new destinations.

In conclusion, we want to express how much we admire, respect, and value you, mid-career teachers, and all you bring to the teaching profession. You bring not only expertise, but also heart, into your practice. You are confident in your teaching practice yet remain curious, open to learning and unlearning (Wink, 2011), or, as we suggest, packing, unpacking, and repacking your professional backpacks. Now, we invite you to delve into the next chapter in which we explore critical thinking, passion, and work-life balance.

Journal Prompt: Unpacking Assumptions

Brookfield's (2017) four lenses provide a useful structure to examine our assumptions. Each of the four lenses asks those close to our practice to provide feedback that we may or may not want to hear. As you individually explore these lenses, be courageous to hear what others have to say and deeply consider what you can learn, unlearn, and relearn from this new information.

Learners' Eyes—As your students learn from you, you also learn from your students. What do you want to know about their learning experiences—that you do not already know? Some possible questions are:

- How do they feel about a specific unit or lesson?
- What interests them or motivates them?
- What are their fears and hopes?
- What difficulties get in the way of their learning, or what supports help them learn?

    List your question(s):
-
-
-
-

Colleagues' Perceptions—You also learn from other teachers—your colleagues. How can their expertise and experience inform your practice? What questions do you have for your colleagues? Some examples include:

- How do they negotiate the evolving nature of classroom dynamics?
- How do they cope with students who appear to resist learning?
- How do they manage their interactions with or responses to a particular student, parent, another colleague, or administrator?
- Where do they find sources of hope when dealing with a difficult teaching day?

    List your question(s):
-
-
-
-

Personal Experience—Naturally, you can reflect on your own experience with teaching, schooling, and life. How are your personal learning experiences influencing your teaching practice? Consider these questions as you form your own:

- What engaged or bored me as a learner?
- What approaches or activities helped or inhibited my learning?
- What were my successes or challenges with different types of assessment?
- What could prompt me to participate or decide not to in an activity?
  List your question(s):
-
-
-
-

Theory—As a mid-career teacher, you know a lot about teaching. We contend that a theory or theories, whether named or not, influence your teaching practice in some way. Perhaps it is time to reflect on these theories or consider others. Here are a few questions to prompt your own:

- What theories or theories did I hear the most about in my preparation program?
- Which of these theories makes sense to me now?
- What theories did I initially embrace that no longer resonate with me?
- Which theories align with my own worldview?
  List your question(s):
-
-
-
-

References

Archer, M. (2012). *The reflexive imperative in late modernity*. Cambridge University Press.

Beach, H., & Strijack, T. N. (2020). *Reclaiming our students: Why children are more anxious, aggressive, and shut down than ever—And what we can do about it*. Page Two.

Bolton, G. (2009). Write to learn: Reflective practice writing. *InnovAiT: Education and Inspiration for General Practice, 2*(12), 752–754. https://doi.org/10.1093/innovait/inp105

Bolton, G., & Delderfield, R. (2018). *Reflective practice: Writing and professional development* (5th ed.). SAGE Publications Ltd.

Boud, D. (2001). Using journal writing to enhance reflective practice. *New Directions for Adult and Continuing Education, 2001*(90), 9–18. https://doi.org/10.1002/ace.16

Brookfield, S. (1998). Critically reflective practice. *Journal of Continuing Education in the Health Professions, 18*(4), 197–205. https://doi.org/10.1002/chp.1340180402

Brookfield, S. D. (2017). *Becoming a critically reflective teacher* (2nd ed.). Jossey-Bass.

Brown, K. M. (2004). Leadership for social justice and equity: Weaving a transformative framework and pedagogy. *Educational Administration Quarterly, 40*(1), 77–108. https://doi.org/10.1177/0013161x03259147

Caprar, D. V., Walker, B. W., & Ashforth, B. E. (2022). The dark side of strong identification in organizations: A conceptual review. *Academy of Management Annals, 16*(2), 759–805. https://doi.org/10.5465/annals.2020.0338

Fernyhough, C. (2016). *The voices within: The history and science of how we talk to ourselves.* Basic Books.

Feucht, F. C., Lunn Brownlee, J., & Schraw, G. (2017). Moving beyond reflection: Reflexivity and epistemic cognition in teaching and teacher education. *Educational Psychologist, 52*(4), 234–241. https://doi.org/10.1080/00461520.2017.1350180

Kennedy, M. M. (2019). How we learn about teacher learning. *Review of Research in Education, 43*(1), 138–162. https://doi.org/10.3102/0091732X19838970

Mezirow, J. (2009). Transformative learning theory. In J. Mezirow, E. W. Taylor, & Associates (Eds.), *Transformative learning in practice: Insights from community, workplace, and higher education* (pp. 18–32). Jossey–Bass.

Muhammad, G. (2023). *Unearthing joy: A guide to culturally and historically responsive teaching and learning.* Scholastic Inc.

Oleś, P. K., Brinthaupt, T. M., Dier, R., & Polak, D. (2020). Types of inner dialogues and functions of self-talk: Comparisons and implications. *Frontiers in Psychology, 11*, Article 227, 1–10. https://doi.org/10.3389/fpsyg.2020.00227

Sprott, R. A. (2019). Factors that foster and deter advanced teachers' professional development. *Teaching and Teacher Education, 77*, 321–331. https://doi.org/10.1016/j.tate.2018.11.001

Wink, J. (2011). *Critical pedagogy: Notes from the real world.* Pearson.

Wu, Y., & Crocco, O. (2019). Critical reflection in leadership development. *Industrial and Commercial Training, 51*(7/8), 409–420. https://doi.org/10.1108/ICT-03-2019-0022

7

Critical Thinking, Passion, and Work-Life Balance

Teaching is a passion. Finding a work-life balance can be difficult because of the illusion that passion should be tireless. Teachers are problem-solvers. We answer upward of 1,500 questions in a single day. This level of interaction with students, teachers, and parents can be exhausting. In this chapter, we will discuss the role that critical thinking plays in moving professional conversation toward a productive end. We will also address the cycle of working in a passion-driven environment and the reality of exhaustion. We end with a practical discussion of three types of work-life balance for the purpose of identifying how we manage our personal and professional lives.

We have great respect for the author, bell hooks. Her career in teaching and writing centered on the exploration of passion, vulnerability, and personal growth. hooks (2014) wrote:

> ...*without the capacity to think critically about ourselves and our lives, none of us would be able to* move forward, to change, to grow. ... *Engaged pedagogy has been essential to my development as an intellectual, as a teacher/professor because* the heart of this approach to learning is critical thinking. *Conditions of* radical openness *exist in any learning situation where students and teachers* celebrate their abilities *to think critically, to engage in* pedagogical praxis.
>
> (p. 202)

DOI: 10.4324/9781003586241-10

In other words, critical thinking grows our capacity as teachers to be open to new ideas about students, teaching, and learning.

Critical Thinking

hooks' (2014) writing challenges the reader to think deeply about the message their teaching, classroom setup, curriculum, and management sends to students. It is through a critical examination of our work that we can challenge our assumptions and clarify our higher goals such as creating a learning community, promoting and protecting diversity and inclusivity.

We have chosen five themes from her book *Teaching Critical Thinking: Practical Wisdom* (hooks, 2014). In previous chapters, we discussed Brookfield's (2017) critical *reflective practice* model. One of the four ways to challenge our assumptions is through theory; hooks' book is an example of using theory to shed some light on our long-held ideas about teaching. Keep in mind that the purpose is not to agree with a theory or an author but to try on these alternative views, see what fits and what does not, and then recreate or reorganize our thinking and actions. The role of mutual mentoring as mid-career teacher-friends involves the evolution of our teacher identity, pedagogical knowledge, and purpose for teaching. Passion keeps us in the game for the first four years; however, depth, courage, and creativity keep us in the game for the long run.

Purpose and Passion. What is our goal or desired outcome for teaching? Those passionate about teaching might say they want to "change lives." Others may value being on the same schedule as their children. Some love their content and want to share that love with others. There are many motivations to teach. We have devoted the next section of this chapter to the topic of passion.

Telling the Story. We love a good story, whether it is a book, an article, or a conversation. Reading and listening to other people's (2017) stories provide context to think about our own story. Another of Brookfield's (2017) reflective elements is *autobiography*. When we listen to someone's story, we understand them better and can ask them questions to clarify our understanding or learn something new. As a teacher-friend, it also allows us to push their thinking about their own story.

Telling our story can be through small anecdotes during common planning or a team or committee meeting. Sharing our stories makes us vulnerable and brings clarity to the elusive. But the depth of autobiography might come in long trekking conversations or writing in our journals as we process new ideas, old ideas, and possibilities. hook (2014) states that stories heal.

Hearing a Story. Everyone has a story. Active listening makes us more empathic and patient and refocuses our attention on the speaker rather than on ourselves. Listening to teacher-friends can also impact collaboration and collegiality. We learn through stories and from others' experiences. Stories help us remember important ideas and help us transfer information in and out of new contexts. Imagine a trek where only one person talks the whole way or there is only chit-chat for miles. This would make the trek less rich and merely a long walk.

Imagination and Creative Thinking. Teaching is expected to involve designing creative ways for students to learn content and skills and demonstrate their understanding. However, we use imagination and creative thinking to guide a teacher's critical thinking about their work, goals, and decision-making. As hooks (2014) said, "We need imagination to illuminate those spaces not covered by data, facts or proven information" (p. 59). The cliché that we are only limited by our imaginations holds true within the context of this book. There is a distinct difference between logistical constraints such as a bell schedule or scripted curriculum and an unpacked assumption that we default to in our decision-making, personally and professionally. Imagination and creative thinking dovetail perfectly with critical thinking about an issue. Imagination and creative thinking challenge us to back away to gain perspective on the task or problem at hand. Good talk can spark ideas that would otherwise not have occurred to us, provide alternative stories or narratives, inspire, or provide hope.

Imagination and creative thinking are not cute or light. hooks (2014) stated, "much intellectual work embraces the art of the possible; it is like an archaeological process where one goes deep in search of truths that may constantly change as new information come to light" (p. 139). Again, this is why the trekking metaphor works for mid-career teacher development. Trekking is a one-way destination, parts are uphill, and others are downhill; the landscape is changing along the way; and what we have packed is utilized when appropriate or in a way that we had not anticipated. For example, duct tape can be wrapped around your water bottle. You can use this one item to cover a blister, repair a backpack, or waterproof a hat. The only limit is necessity and your imagination in the problem-solving process.

Practical Wisdom. The combination of passion, imagination, good talk, and purpose is that in the integration of all these attributes of teaching is the development of practical wisdom. The engagement of reflection and critical thinking is a "mindful awareness which heightens our capacity to live fully and well" (hooks, 2014, p. 185). hooks (2014) weaves together the idea that critical thinking and practical wisdom are intertwined with theory and knowledge that build experiences. Teaching as an integrated person takes all this experience and brings it into the classroom.

In conclusion, personal and professional depth comes in stages in fits and starts. A recognizable emotional or intellectual itch or discomfort signals when it is time to learn, reflect, and change. In the next section, we discuss the passion for teaching or being a teacher. It is a hot topic today in many work scenarios, but little talked about is the cost of passion. A discussion of passion, exhaustion, and recovery will add to understanding the ebb and flow of the school year and a sustainable teaching career.

Passion, Exhaustion, and Recovery

The trekking metaphor implies a long, interesting, challenging, and enjoyable journey. However, it is unreasonable to trek without rest, snacks, Band-Aids, Gatorade, and companionship. All the excitement in the world would not sustain our minds and bodies over the long term. It is with this mindset that a discussion of passion, exhaustion, and recovery is anchored.

Passion and Exhaustion

Teachers are known for being passionate professionals, for learning and students, their specialized content. Passion is a popular concept in the hiring process. Passion is attributed to employees who work longer hours, stay in a position for a longer period, and have a positive outlook.

> *Particularly for teachers who entered the profession feeling passionate about making a difference, remaining passionate in a context of professional and cultural ambiguity is a formidable challenge at every career stage, perhaps most particularly for those new to the profession.*
>
> (Fogelgarn & Burns, 2020, p. 495)

Passionate teaching includes a commitment to the joy of discovery, the welfare and learning of students, and belief in the benefit that education brings to students' lives and families (van Manen, 1991). Teachers are not born passionate about the profession. Many find their vocation and bring passion to the position to do well and see the learning and development in their students. According to Day (2004), passion for teaching includes believing every child can learn and a commitment to seeing them grow. However, passion can ebb and flow as a response to professional and personal circumstances. To care deeply about the learning and success of others requires energy, commitment, bravery, and confidence. Teaching is an "emotionally vulnerable context" in which students learn.

Competing ideals make teaching and learning tenuous. The first is that teaching is heart work. Second is the ebb and flow between teaching and learning is rarely gentle and steady. Third is that learning is not predictable but rather a student's process toward becoming an adult and being independent. It is also no surprise that students respond to teachers who believe they care about them (Noddings, 2015). However, passion comes at a price, and that price can be exhaustion and burnout. What we find so interesting about passion is that it is an emotional asset and thus also an emotional burden.

Jachimowicz et al. (2018) defined passion as "a strong feeling toward a personally meaningful value or preference that motivates intentions and behaviors to express that value or preference" (p. 9981). When people asked us what we do and we answered "I teach middle school" or "I do research about successful middle school practice," people inevitably said, "Oh, bless your heart. I would hate to teach middle school." However, for us, it has been our sweet spot, where we find flow. We cannot imagine working anywhere else. Middle school students and teachers are home for us.

An old saying is that "if you do what you love you'll never work a day in your life." We don't know about you, but we work every day as teachers. In fact, finding work that aligns with our passion and is sustainable over time is difficult; teachers seem to be lucky in finding their passion but less effective at sustaining it, considering the realities of the job. This is particularly true for teachers and other service professions (Nielsen & Colbert, 2022). In other words, pursuing your passion can be challenging and draining, which is rarely how popular culture packages this gift. Our goal in defining and demystifying passion is to provide a clear understanding and expectations around us, using our passion to teach.

Bredehorst et al. (2024) paint a clear picture using the transactional stress model and evaluated the individual's feelings about their passion at work. It appears that if a person is highly passionate one day or for a project, there is a toll to pay in subsequent days. In the case of teachers, because we can be passion-driven, that passion is or becomes part of our identity as teachers. Therefore, the toll can interfere or spill over into other parts of life. This is work-life balance. Bredehorst et al. continue to say that passion-driven employees internalize the passion for daily work, defined as "whether they are feeling in control of or controlled by their passion" (p. 365). They conclude that to leverage the pursuit of passion against the result of exhaustion takes a daily self-managing process using personal and organizational structures. They suggest more specifically that:

> *Unless employees adequately regulate their passion on any given day—higher levels of passion will lead them to invest more time and energy into their work, decreasing their psychological detachment from work after the workday, and consequently resulting in higher levels of emotional exhaustion the next day.*
>
> (p. 364)

These authors report that if organizations want to benefit from hiring and retaining passionate employees, they need to support those employees in managing their resources and recovery daily. Employees can self-regulate:

- *after* a demanding day if they have less autonomous control of their passion,
- *during* a high demand day if they have more autonomous control of their passion,
- create a *practice* so that a demanding day doesn't result in being exhausted, and

The more self-regulated passion is at work, the less the recovery process spills over into home.

The outcome of this line of research on passion and exhaustion begs the question as to "why can some employees sustain passion over a longer period of time while others lose their passion more quickly?" An additional factor is that passion varies as the work tasks change and what the employee cares most about at the time. Therefore, the person who is most passionate about the work is likely to be the least exhausted by the work (Lavoie et al., 2021). These employees feel like they have the resources to complete the task and identify fewer risks.

Recovery

How do teachers and others who work in a passion-driven career recover? Did you even know that recovery needed to be part of the cycle? Recovery means "unwinding and restoration processes during which a person's strain level that has increased as a reaction to a stressor or any other demand returns to its pre-stressor level" (Sonnentag et al., 2017, p. 366).

Recovery after a highly passionate day requires employees to switch gears; however, this can be easier said than done. Many times, if a practice of self-regulation is not in place of work life bleeds into home life, which does not allow the time or detachment necessary to rejuvenate for the next day. Four ways to recover are:

- psychological detachment from work, whereby

- relaxation is participating in a practice that is calming both physically and mentally—such as meditation or exercise.
- mastery is the feeling of success associated with a growing set of skills that help coping and recovery.
- control refers to having a sense of agency through which to process a stressful day (Ouyang et al., 2019)

The lack of a passion intermission results in an employee being less passionate the next day. West et al. (2021) found that a weekend may not hold the recovery time necessary for highly passionate people because Saturday and Sunday are filled with the demands of home and family. They suggested that additional days off tended to be scheduled for more open-ended relaxation. A microbreak is taking a short break during the workday to re-energize. Three suggested strategies for taking a microbreak include:

1. taking a walk, talking with a friend or colleague, or exercising,
2. organizing and scheduling, reflective practice, or collaboration to offset isolation. Some research found that a combination of microbreaks and work-related breaks proved most beneficial—for example, walking while collaborating, and
3. a private break which might include reading, listening to music, or using social media.

Physical and social activities were found to be more restorative during the workday (Kim et al., 2017). Research revealed that employees who intentionally plan and take breaks experience lower levels of fatigue and stress (Blasche et al., 2017). de Bloom et al. (2018) found that people using used physical and social activities reported higher psychological detachment from work and more relaxation, mastery, and control than those who were inactive. The people in this category were also found to attend more creative and cultural activities. High-energy recovery activities showed to have a greater reset value for the next day than low-energy recovery activities. For example, exercise was more effective than watching television. "Taken together, research has shown that recovery experiences such as psychological detachment from work, relaxation, mastery, and control are related to better well-being and more favorable affective states at bedtime and at the start of the next morning" (Sonnentag et al., 2022, p. 38).

Teachers understand that working with students is an emotional process. Teachers are known to be resilient, courageous, and intrinsically motivated and committed to doing what is best for students. Therefore, it is reasonable to provide support, including significant financial, structural, and spiritual investment (Fogelgarn & Burns, 2020). Thus, teachers need the restoration of their emotional energy and passion.

Hydration Station: Passionate Teachers

The passion for teaching has been an important topic for writers and researchers for more than 50 years. They praise teachers for embodying elements of care, empathy, courage, and hope. They also acknowledge that agency and resilience are required for teachers to be passionate about teaching and effective over time.

- Good teaching is known to include pedagogical knowledge, personal attributes, content knowledge, and empathy (Palmer, 1998).
- Teacher identity does not distinguish between professional identity and personal passion (Nias, 1999).
- Teachers are passionate and devote themselves to their work (Day, 2004).
- Teachers care about their students through connections in the classroom, student achievement, and well-being. Care is a part of the professional requirement (Noddings, 1992).
- When the person and the professional activities of life blend seamlessly—it is called "flow" (Csikszentmihalyi, 1990).
- Teachers embody qualities like care, courage, fairness, kindness, honesty, and perseverance (Noddings, 2003; Palmer, 2004).
- Teacher identity and agency are central to their motivation, commitment, well-being, and capacity to teach to their best (Day & Lee, 2011).
- For teachers to lead and teach, they must understand their emotions and the emotions of others to manage the learning environment. Good teaching requires the connection of emotion with self-knowledge" (Zembylas, 2003, p. 213).
- Teachers must be hopeful and resilient and lead, and to be a good and effective teacher over time requires hopefulness and resilience and the ability to identify, demanding circumstances and be flexible in different contexts (Day & Gu, 2013).

To summarize, teaching is not for the faint of heart. Teaching is a deeply personal profession in which identity, emotion, and training influence the learning of students every day.

Micki on Passion, Exhaustion, and Recovery

I fell in love with teaching seventh-grade students in a junior high school, though I had only been prepared to teach early childhood and elementary-age children. These young adolescents captured my heart and brought so much joy to my professional life. I found it so easy to teach life science to these youth who came from underserved and economically strapped communities. Perhaps it was because they were so eager to learn about their developing bodies and the natural world around them. Or perhaps it had a lot to do with Merilee Harrison, a veteran science teacher, who showed me the ropes of planning, organization, and routines. Everything in my teaching day hummed along beautifully. I was also challenged to figure out how to reach and teach students who had difficulty reading any of the science materials. I tried grouping and regrouping yet soon realized that I needed to know more. So back to the university I went in search of practices to support my students with learning differences. Though I found it demanding to take master's classes in the evening and work full time, I was chasing my passion to meet the needs of all young adolescents in my classroom.

After securing my degree in special education, I accepted a position teaching adolescents who had been diagnosed with specific learning disabilities. The position led me to teach youth in grades 10–12 in another inner-city school. Challenged by school size and the invisibility of my special needs students, I soon transferred to a junior high school where I would teach for the next 11 years. Yet, I loved the work; I frequently hit the wall. I focused on teaching and supporting my young adolescent learners, but the workload was exhaustive given the IEPs, annual reviews, re-evaluations, and compliance meetings. During these years, I married and had a daughter—two high points and the joys of my life. Thus, I struggled like many teachers to balance the responsibilities of family life and professional life. I was burning the candle at both ends so I could serve my students well and be fully present for my own family.

My professional life began to shift when I accepted my district's invitation to join a cadre of professional development specialists charged with an initiative to transition our junior highs into middle schools. Working with my vice principal, Sue Allen, and two district specialists, Elizabeth Wilson and Lynn Brennan, was a turning point because each of these women leaders valued me and what I could bring to the initiative. Soon after, I changed schools to serve as the curriculum integration specialist at a high-tech, magnet middle school. So, not only was I part of the district's initiative, but I also had a new type of teaching position. Working with passionate middle school teachers and young adolescents became part of my professional identity. And, the next thing I know, I was beginning a doctoral program ... I had found my way.

Karen on Passion, Exhaustion, and Recovery

I come from a long line of teachers, and I have always known I would be a teacher. In seventh grade, I had Mr. Warwick for Life Science, and that was what I wanted to do. This was solidified by Mr. Lee in ninth-grade Biology and Dr. Mogenson in Botany in college. In retrospect, all these teachers were passionate about their content and students. Ironically, they were also all men in a male-dominated field. My first job was at Mount Elden Middle School in Flagstaff, Arizona. While I had no middle school specific training, I immediately knew that eighth graders were my people. I subsequently taught there for 12 years. I loved the highs of teaching; when a lesson went better than expected, students really understood the objective, and my relationship with them was positive, fun, and what I had always imagined.

I wonder if it was "what I imagined" teaching to be, added to the weight of teaching. Exhaustion in my teaching was real. I planned on my own but had a middle school team that met to discuss kids and integrated unit planning once a week. It was difficult to generate every lesson for every day by myself. I was also hard on myself, wondering what I could do better. I worked in a diverse school that required learning "Spanish for Teachers," the beginning of state testing and its impact on curriculum and instruction, and teaming with one very difficult English teacher. I would often go home after school and take a two-hour nap just to decompress. While I loved teaching and the students, the job was demanding, constant, and tearful at times.

For me recovery came in my teacher-friend, Michele. We met when she was a substitute teacher in the classroom across the hall. She eventually became the chemistry teacher at the feeder high school. We would walk once a week after school and talk about life and work. I also started a doctoral program in curriculum and instruction, which took the next three years but added so much to my depth of knowledge in the classroom. It was absolutely no fun but also filled with a deep thirst for challenging my mind, my endurance, and my self-concept. Recovery was not restful for me; it was found in a challenge that set of course for my next professional move.

In the next section, we discuss work-life balance by identifying that there are several theoretical frameworks for work-life balance and that, while popular culture talks about balance in generalities, we invite you to consider three frameworks that might resonate with your current circumstances, personality, or priorities.

Exploring Work-Life Balance

Teachers are historically known for taking papers home to grade, planning on the weekends, and working late to complete their tasks. These are among the leading causes for teachers leaving the profession. This is an important topic to build in reflexive practice—examining assumptions about what is really needed to be successful, how to establish healthy boundaries, and create a sustainable, productive, and edifying practice. Work-life balance is about helping individuals match their behavior to their values (Gurvis & Patterson, 2005). There are several theories about work-life balance, and we imagine that as teachers we grow in and out of different theoretical frameworks, as we mature, become experts in our fields, and as our families grow and change.

Kirchmeyer (2000) defined work-life balance as having the necessary resources such as energy, time, and commitment to make the major aspects of life enjoyable. Another perspective is one that is situational, ever-changing. Kofodimos (1993) described situational balance as:

> ... finding the allocation of time and energy that fits your values and needs, making conscious choices about how to structure your life and integrating inner needs and outer demands and involves honoring and living by your deepest personal qualities, values, and goals.
>
> (p. 8)

There are several different and evolving definitions of work-life balance. In our review of the literature, we identified four theories that had illustrative elements that help us identify balance and imbalance more specifically. Understanding these multiple theories also provided insight that not only are there differing definitions but that work-life balance is a very large bucket. We discuss work as one domain and life as another. Next, we present three theories: spillover, compensation, and boundary. We hope you find a model that resonates and helps you better understand how you personally think about balance.

Spillover Theory

Work-life balance came to the forefront in the 1960s and 1970s due to the large influx of women into the workplace. As the name implies, spillover theory explains that there is no defined line between work and home. Spillover suggests that "workers carry the emotions, attitudes, skills and behaviors that they establish at work into their family life and vice versa" (Rincy & Panchanatham, 2014). Men were found to view spillover from work into family, while women found spillover from family into work (Pleck, 1995). Spillover theory is inclusive of both the positive and negative effects and thus appears to be boundary-less. However, work-family conflict is a predictor of intent to quit a job that does not provide balance (Yildiz et al., 2021).

Positive spillover refers to positive effects in either work or home transfer over to the other. An example of a positive spillover could be an employee receiving a promotion or recognition and those positive feelings influencing their home. Negative spillover refers to negative effects in either work or home that transfer over into the other. An example of a negative spillover could be an employee who is in the process of getting a divorce in their personal life and that negatively affects their work performance.

Compensation Theory
Compensation theory represents the idea that if a person is unfulfilled in one domain (work or home) they may overcompensate in the other domain. Interestingly, because work and home are shared experiences, Rincy and Panchanatham (2014) suggest that if work is negative then home is positive and vice versa. Compensation theory is like a teeter-totter. The first is that a person decreases their participation in the negative domain and increases their participation in the positive domain. One element of experiencing positivity in a domain is through receiving rewards in areas that bring them satisfaction.

Border Theory
Border theory refers to "satisfaction and good functioning at work and at home, with a minimum of role conflict" (Clark, 2000, p. 751). This theory focuses on how people make, change, and hold boundaries so that they can better understand, simplify, and categorize their life experiences. The goal is to minimize the transition between work and home. Boundary theory views work and home as separate domains that affect one another (Clark, 2000). Boundaries can be strong and inflexible, regarded as border keepers, while border crossers are more likely to be weak and blended.

In conclusion, organizations such as schools can support teachers by empowering them to within their passion and their ability to recharge emotionally to decrease the experience of burnout. Some leaders may use passion as an excuse to increase the workload and responsibilities of an already overloaded employee. According to Sonnentag et al. (2022), leaders should be aware of high passion days and support the employee (for example, teachers) in the subsequent recovery day by not adding more tasks. For example, in teaching, principals should encourage teachers to work within their contract hours and seek out ways for work not to spill over into time at home and ways to leave the emotional work at school. The outcome is then to have an increased reservoir of passion to pull from and a few days of exhaustion.

Passion, recovery, and work-life balance are all part of sustaining our energy as mid-career teachers and professionals. With each of these notions, there is no one-size solution. As mentioned in previous chapters, knowing ourselves better through dialogue and practice takes time, planning, quiet moments, and action. As we explore our assumptions about our teaching, students, and our personal lives, we learn to be brave, resilient, and creative. We drew on these attributes when we chose trekking as the metaphor for mid-career mutual mentoring. In the next section we draw parallels between mutual mentoring and trekking. We insist that trekking is a macro-recovery idea that can keep teachers engaged, satisfied, and curious.

Journal Prompt: Boundaries Are Like Sunscreen
Within our metaphor, we liken boundaries to sunscreen. While trekking it is important to use sunscreen to protect our skin and our fun. Sunburn can be painful, interrupt sleep, and make it impossible to carry a backpack. Much like in life, boundaries serve the same purpose as sunscreen. Boundaries can protect us from "too much" of anything (working too much, saying yes too much, complaining too much, taking on too much). In the end, a lack of boundaries, whether personal and professional, can exhaust us and make us miserable.

Consider the following type of boundaries that are important to teachers and reflect on how you might "apply" stronger limits in these areas. How can you, as teacher-friends, determine how to have more control over your schedule, both personally and professionally?

Time Boundaries
- Do you have an end-of-the-day routine that results in your leaving at the end of your contract time?
- Do you use your individual preparation period to complete tasks during school hours, so you don't have to do them at home?
- Do you volunteer only for activities or meetings that you are passionate about attending?
- Do you have a strong "no"?
- Do you have time for the activities you enjoy doing outside of school?

Task Boundaries
- Do you grade every paper? Can you find ways to implement Learning Management System tools to grade for you?
- Do you refuse to be voluntold to attend IEPs, committee meetings, or other obligations? We encourage you to have a phrase close at hand to use such as "I appreciate your offer, but I need to focus on my current commitments."
- Do you bring work stress home?
- Is multi-tasking in my best interest? Is it truly efficient?

Teacher-Friend Benefits to Setting Boundaries and Sunscreen

A teacher-friend can:

- Put sunscreen on your back, where you can't reach. In a similar fashion, teacher-friends can help you hold your boundaries when you are likely to bend.
- Remind you to reapply your boundary or sunscreen, like leaving school at the end of the contract time.
- Tell you when you are burned, literally and metaphorically. Sometimes we cannot tell this for ourselves.

It is not selfish to set healthy boundaries at work or at home. In fact, the consequences of not setting boundaries lead to burnout and frustration not only for you but those around you. Much like sunscreen, honoring the boundaries you have set for yourself will change or need to be reapplied from time to time. In the same way, depending on the weather, the SPF of sunscreen changes. Work-life balance, supported by strong yet flexible boundaries, can improve the overall quality of life, increase job satisfaction, and lower stress.

Conclusion

Teaching is a career choice that is borne from the heart and fills the soul. The daily work and constraints of teaching can easily erode passion and require recovery. Mid-career can feel like being too far in to quit and too far to go to sustain the energy for work. It takes meaningful conversations and repetitive practice with teacher-friends to grow a habit of joy that is sustainable. There are many values to going on a trek. Some include:

- physical health,
- stress reduction,
- mental health,
- connection to nature,
- personal growth, and
- community building.

In terms of our metaphor that mid-career teachers can mentor each other as teacher-friends, we can see trekking with teacher-friends as professional development. We can:

- exercise (pun intended) their resilience through reflective practice,
- pack, unpack, and repack—what is necessary to have on hand and what to set down,
- process frustrates more quickly and productively,
- stay in teaching and advocate for the profession,
- create positive habits that increase and sustain intellectual and professional development over time, and
- design semi-permeable boundaries that allow them to find a work-life balance that sustains them, adjusts them, and evaluate their effectiveness over time.

The long game is to create a work-life balance that changes and adjusts to the everyday demands of work and family. bell hooks (2014) challenges us to be vulnerable. Passion requires vulnerability and is risky but in turn opens new creative pathways that can refresh and renew us. In the next section, Venturing, we invite you to plan your own adventure.

References

Blasche, G., Pasalic, S., Bauböck, V.-M., Haluza, D., & Schoberberger, R. (2017). Effects of rest-break intention on rest-break frequency and work-related fatigue. *Human Factors: The Journal of the Human Factors and Ergonomics Society, 59*(2), 289–298. https://doi.org/10.1177/0018720816671605

Bredehorst, J., Krautter, K., Meuris, J., & Jachimowicz, J. M. (2024). The challenge of maintaining passion for work over time: A daily perspective on passion and emotional exhaustion. *Organization Science, 35*(1), 364–386. https://doi.org/10.1287/orsc.2023.1673

Clark, S. C. (2000). Work/family border theory: A new theory of work. Family balance. *Human Relations, 53*(6), 747–770. https://psycnet.apa.org/doi/10.1177/0018726700536001

Csikszentmihalyi, M. (1990). *Flow: The psychology of optimal experience.* Harper & Row.

Day, C. (2004). *A passion for teaching.* University of Nottingham. https://doi.org/10.4324/9780203464342

Day, C., & Gu, Q. (2013). *Resilient teachers, resilient schools: Building and sustaining quality in testing times.* Routledge. https://doi.org/10.4324/9780203578490

Day, C., & Lee, J. C. K. (Eds.). (2011). *New understandings of teacher's work: Emotions and educational change.* Springer.

de Bloom, J., Rantanen, J., Temen, T. S., & Kinnunen, U. (2018). Longitudinal leisure activity profiles and their associations with recovery experiences and job performance. *Leisure Science, 40,* 151–173. https://doi.org/10.1080/01490400.2017.1356254

Fogelgarn, R., & Burns, E. A. (2020). What constrains passionate teaching? A heuristic exploration. *Issues in Educational Research, 30*(2), 493–511.

Gurvis, J., & Patterson, G. (2005). Balancing act: Finding equilibrium between work and life. *Leadership in Action, 24,* 4–10. https://doi.org/10.1002/lia.1091

hooks, B. (2014). *Teaching to transgress.* Routledge. https://doi.org/10.4324/9780203700280

Jachimowicz, J. M., Wihler, A., Bailey, E. R., & Galinsky, A. D. (2018). Why grit requires perseverance and passion to positively predict performance. *Proceedings of the National Academy of Sciences, 115*(40), 9980–9985. https://doi.org/10.31234/osf.io/6y5xr

Kim, S., Park, Y., & Niu, Q. (2017). Micro-break activity at work to recovery from daily work demands. *Journal of Organizational Behavior, 38,* 28–44. https://doi.org/10.1002/job.2109

Kirchmeyer, C. (2000). Work-life initiatives: Greed or benevolence regarding workers' time? In C. L. Cooper, & D. M. Rousseau (Eds.), *Trends in organizational behavior, Vol. 7. Time in organizational behavior* (pp. 79–93). Wiley & Sons.

Kofodimos, J. R. (1993). *Balancing act: How managers can integrate successful careers and fulfilling personal lives.* Jossey-Bass.

Lavoie, C. E., Vallerand, R. J., & Verner-Filion, J. (2021). Passion and emotions: The mediating role of cognitive appraisals. *Psychology of Sport and Exercise, 54,* 101907. https://doi.org/10.1016/j.psychsport.2021.101907

Nias, J. (1999). Teachers' moral purposes: Stress, vulnerability, and strength. In R. Vandenberghe, & A. M. Huberman (Eds.), *Understanding and preventing teacher burnout: A sourcebook of international research and practice* (pp. 223–237). Cambridge University Press.

Nielsen, J. D., & Colbert, A. E. (2022). It's not always sunny in relationally rich jobs: The influence of negative beneficiary contact. *Academy of Management Journal, 65*(6), 1894–1922. https://doi.org/10.5465/amj.2019.1288

Noddings, N. (1992). In defense of caring. *The Journal of Clinical Ethics, 3*(1), 15–18. https://doi.org/10.1086/jce199203103

Noddings, N. (2003). Is teaching a practice? *Journal of Philosophy of Education, 37*(2), 241–251. https://doi.org/10.1111/1467-9752.00323

Noddings, N. (2015). *The challenge to care in schools* (2nd ed.). Teachers College Press.

Ouyang, K., Cheng, B. H., Lam, W., & Parker, S. K. (2019). Enjoy your evening, be proactive tomorrow: How off-job experiences shape daily proactivity. *Journal of Applied Psychology, 104*, 1003–1019. https://psycnet.apa.org/doi/10.1037/apl0000391

Palmer, P. J. (1998). Leading from within. In L. C. Spears (Ed.), *Insights on leadership: Service, stewardship, spirit, and servant-leadership* (pp. 197–208). Wiley.

Palmer, P. J. (2004). Teaching with heart and soul: Reflections on spirituality in teacher education. *Journal of Teacher Education, 54*(5), 376–385. https://doi.org/10.1177/0022487103257359

Pleck, J. H. (1995). The gender role strain paradigm: An update. In R. F. Levant, & W. S. Pollack (Eds.), *A new psychology of men* (pp. 11–32). Basic Books/Hachette Book Group.

Rincy, V. M., & Panchanatham, N. (2014). Work life balance: A short review of the theoretical and contemporary concepts. *Continental Journal of Social Sciences, 7*(1), 1–24.

Sonnentag, S., Cheng, B. H., & Parker, S. L. (2022). Recovery from work: Advancing the field toward the future. *Annual Review of Organizational Psychology and Organizational Behavior, 9*(1), 3360. https//doi.org/10.1146/annurev-orgpsych-012420-091355

Sonnentag, S., Venz, L., & Casper, A. (2017). Advances in recovery research: What have we learned? What should be done next? *Journal of Occupational Health Psychology, 22*, 365–380. https://doi.org/10.1037/ocp0000079

van Manen, M. (1991). *The tact of teaching: The meaning of pedagogical thoughtfulness.* State University of New York Press.

West, C., Mogilner, C., & DeVoe, S. E. (2021). Happiness from treating the weekend like a vacation. *Social Psychological and Personality Science, 12*(3), 346–356. https://doi.org/10.1177/1948550620916080

Yildiz, B., Yildiz, H., & Ayaz Arda, O. (2021). Relationship between work–family conflict and turnover intention in nurses: A meta-analytic review. *Journal of Advanced Nursing, 77*(8), 3317–3330. https://doi.org/10.1111/jan.14846

Zembylas, M. (2003). Emotions and teacher identity: A poststructural perspective. *Teachers and Teaching, 9*(3), 213–238. https://doi.org/10.1080/13540600309378

Part 3

Venturing

8

Preparing for an Adventure

It is time to figure out what type of professional growth will invigorate your teaching, challenge your intellect, and keep you in the teaching game. We focus this chapter on discerning what you are interested in pursuing and what is the best timeframe. In the first section, we discuss the aspect of the adventure. The second section is about choosing the best time to start and how long the project will take. The third section is about what to pack so that your pursuit is successful.

Adventure

It is always fun to have something to look forward to doing. Planning a teacher-friend adventure can hold elements of excitement, the unknown, challenges, and changes. Expanding the trekking metaphor, we use the term adventure to invoke the unknown, the "what if." Adventure emphasizes the solitude from the everyday and self-discovery aspects of adventure, where we must rely on inner strength and intuition to navigate through unfamiliar and often challenging circumstances. We can adventure with others, in this case teacher-friends, or on our own.

Adventure is not just about physical exploration but also about the internal journey of growth, learning, and transformation. Stepping into the unknown, while daunting, can lead to profound professional development as well as a deeper understanding of ourselves. In this chapter, we talk about several important factors to consider before starting your mid-career teacher-friend mentoring adventure. The first is choosing a *project* or *destination*. What do you want to learn more about? The second is *timing*, when is the best time of year to begin your project, and how long do you want this to take? The third is *gear*, what do you need to have purchased and packed ahead of time to be comfortable and successful. Gear includes boots, a backpack, a camera, a map, a compass, a magnifying glass, a journal, sunglasses, a journal, and sunscreen. Each of these supports the trekking metaphor and our view of the teacher-friend mentoring process.

Possible Destinations

As a mid-career teacher, you know what kind of in-service experiences you like, learn from, and would recommend to others. Many feel there is nothing worse than a one-size-fits-all approach to professional development. We may prefer to choose to use our time to learn about content area pedagogy or student engagement rather than a broader topic that lacks specifics. There may be topics we no longer need or that are not a high priority. Teacher-friend mentoring is designed with an adult learning framework (Chapter 2). Therefore, it is important to know your priorities well so that you and your partner can make a plan that interests you both, challenges you both, and is engaging.

To help you consider possible destinations, we reveal some of our own preferences through the following reflections. First, we share our thoughts about where we like to trek. Then, we disclose where our own professional development adventures have taken us.

Karen's Thoughts

I would not go trekking just anywhere. I have my preferences which I am willing to stretch but not abandon. For example, I am a mountain girl. I like to go to the ocean but not get in it. I would kayak but not swim. In a similar vein, I love the mountains but will not be sleeping in a tent. I want a bed, coffee, and warmth. I am willing to walk, bike, hike, climb, but not swim, swat at big bugs, or eat weird stuff. I would not make the perfect trekking partner for everyone.

In terms of teaching, I enjoy research-based practices. I appreciate frameworks that give me the opportunity to add in the details for middle grades and science. I love collaborating with teachers who are curious, organized, and kind. In professional development, I want to learn something new, be reminded of something founded in theory, and a practical application of the concept. I want time in the day when I learn something new to grapple with it and discuss where it best fits or will fit.

Micki's Thoughts

I enjoy trekking the trails of the Oregon coast or the California desert, as well as those along mountain rivers and lakes, just about anywhere in the world. That said, I do not like getting too close to the edge of an overlook or anywhere that I may slip and fall. I have a healthy respect for gravity. I am a fair-weather trekker, so I prefer being outdoors in warm and sunny weather, but I am okay if I get wet by an unanticipated downpour. I like to push myself and work up a sweat; I also love to walk slowly and take in the beauty of nature. I want a trekking partner who is open to exploring new places and revisiting favorite spaces, who embraces conversation and silence, and who likes going fast and slow.

In terms of teaching, I often travel with teachers who think like me or those who push me to think in new or different ways. I enjoy being a member of a team … whether with one other teacher or a group of teachers. I thrive on the camaraderie and solidarity I feel with my teacher-friends. I also find I need individual time for thinking, reading, writing, planning, imagining, and reflecting. My solo work, coupled with my teamwork, helps me to grow and follow my passion for teaching.

Trail Talk

Now, it is your turn. Where do you want to go on your trek? Take a few minutes to consider some possible destinations. Then, list where you would like to go with a teacher-friend.

Somewhere familiar:

1.
2.
3.

Somewhere new for both of us:

1.
2.
3.

Somewhere you have been, but I have not been:

1.
2.
3.

These are all important questions to consider ahead of planning a trek. We offer a list of possibilities that begs to be expanded; it is where you begin to personalize the journey. Now that you have listed some ideas about possible destinations, we want to offer you a few more to extend or enhance yours.

- Participate in a professional learning community around content, pedagogy, age-level, or …
- Join a book group with purpose: Brené Brown books, pedagogy, children's literature, young adult literature, and …
- Find a Walk and Talk partners, an exercise program, and …
- Enroll in a program together: master's, doctoral, administrator credential, counseling, English Language Learner certification, National Board Certification, and …

Timing Is Everything

Planning an adventure is exciting. However, choosing the ideal time to begin an adventure is important. It is also important to decide ahead of time how long the adventure should last. Planning a teacher-friend adventure includes a realistic discussion about timing. Do you want to begin a project in August or May? What is the time commitment? If we read a book together, then two months might be great. If you decide to do a pedagogical action research project, then the academic year would be most appropriate. The important point is to make a realistic estimate of the time you will need to start your project, enjoy the process, and end that works for both of you.

We recommend that teacher-friends agree on the length of the project, the activities, and the commitment to get those done. The key is to find the right time of day that works. For example, we are both morning people. We like to write individually before the day gets complicated. We treasure our mornings for quiet reflection, reading, and writing. We write together in the afternoon. This is the best time for us to collaborate, talk, and think together.

If you like quiet mornings to drink coffee and get ready for the day, then you would be wise to set a boundary that identifies what time and for how long you are available and on which days.

Trail Talk

Now is a good time to discuss when and how you and your teacher-friend want to work on your project.

- When do you want to start your project?
- How long do you want to work on this project?

- What day of the week are you both available?
- What time of day will work best for both of you?

The purpose of considering these questions is to help you develop and design for your professional development, for your growth through teacher-friend mentoring, and for your heart and love of teaching. We covered what to pack extensively in Chapter 6. Once you have chosen your adventure, what do you need to make it the best experience for both of you? Here are some places to start:

- A new book
  - Book 1
  - Book 2
  - Book 3
- A class to take—either at the district level or at the university
  - Class 1
  - Class 2
  - Class 3
- Identify a specific student group to work with
  - Group 1
  - Group 2
  - Group 3
- Identify a new pedagogy to learn and implement
  - Pedagogy 1
  - Pedagogy 2
  - Pedagogy 3

Once you have identified when in the academic year you want to start your collaboration, then you will need to decide how long you want this mentoring project to take, and how much time daily or weekly you schedule with each other. Next, it is time to consider what gear you need to achieve your goals and be comfortable along the way.

Trekking Gear: Having the Right Stuff

In Diana Helmuth's (2021) book *How to Suffer Outside. A Beginner's Guide to Hiking and Backpacking,* she makes the point that "in general backpacking gear is ideally as light as possible—in terms of the number of items you carry, their volume and their weight" (p. 31). We agree with this rule of thumb for mentoring gear as well. Choose your topic, a meeting place, buy a journal you will love to write and draw in, a pen that translates your thoughts, a favorite mug, and a teacher-friend. In other words, pack light. Trekking is not "another thing to do"; it is a refreshing walk with good company and the right stuff.

Boots

Boots are a powerful symbol for preparation, resilience, and endurance. We intentionally identified broken-in boots because, as mid-career teachers, having a good pair of comfortable shoes has kept us going. Broken-in boots have molded to our foot shape. They don't give us blisters. They symbolize the strength and readiness required to face life's challenges and navigate difficult terrain. The right shoes can make all the difference in a successful trek or an interrupted trek. We have adjusted to so many factors such as administration, team members, and changing curriculum. We also like adapting to new terrain because every year brings new people, schedules, curriculum, and students.

Our boots help us adapt to new terrain, which means the ability to be flexible and adjust to changing factors, conditions, or environments. The following prompts focus on six areas, related to adaptability. Consider the following when you journal in the future:

- *Communication* with colleagues, parents, and students.
- *Interpersonal skills* to interact with others in a healthy, productive way.
- *Problem-solving* is the ability to analyze a situation and approach a problem systematically.
- *Creative and strategic thinking* is the ability to think in a way that creates new systems and approaches.
- *Teamwork* is your ability to work with your grade level or content area team, professional learning group.
- *Organization* refers to your ability to create systems in which students, parents, and teachers can interact with your class. It also refers to systems that keep you functioning with the least amount of friction regarding time, effort, and repeated attention.

Our boots are loved, well-worn, and comfortable. This has enabled you to teach for more than five years. Your foundation is solid and flexible. In the next section, we discuss your backpack. We previously explained packing, unpacking, and repacking (Chapter 6). Next, apply the trekking metaphor to what items to pack.

What We Bring in Our Backpack

The purpose of Part 1 of this book was to provide you with tools such as self-directed learning, dialogue and practice, and ideas on how and why to journal. These ideas are meant to be the lightweight frame for your backpack. A good frame distributes weight onto the hips, shoulders, and back evenly. A good frame keeps us from getting tired quickly, from the back rubbing in one spot until there is a sore, and allows us to carry more than we thought possible. We like an organized backpack; perhaps you do as well. A backpack symbolizes what we carry with us—whether it's burdens, memories, preparedness, or aspirations. It's about how we navigate life, what we choose to take with us, and how those things shape our journey.

The backpack often represents the things we carry with us in life—both tangible and intangible. In Chapter 6 we described packing, identifying assumptions, and choosing them to examine and possibly redefine them. In this chapter, we are going to focus on the backpack, which represents being prepared. We are equipped to meet challenges, carrying with us what we need to navigate life's obstacles.

What are the characteristics of the best backpack for trekking that supports the teacher-friend mentoring metaphor?

- Lightweight—finding the right teacher-friend
- Multiple compartments—several different ideas that could blend into a project
- Waterproof—we can weather many different situations without it impacting our core
- Multi-purpose—we can use the same backpack for work and play

Your backpack can hold many items for your adventure. We will revisit several items that we discussed in the earlier chapters to remind you way they are important to take with you on your adventure.

Camera
Previously, we suggested that a camera was like data collection. For example, a snapshot of a student's ability at a moment in time. We implied that, as teachers, a camera could capture our professional capabilities in much the same way. You have designed your adventure, so now what moments do you want to capture? The camera in our metaphor can provide a deeper perspective on a situation. If you choose to pack a camera or take along your cell phone, what would you plan to take a picture of to show your progress or record a scenic view?

- Describe your trek.
- Desired outcome.
- What do you want to capture in the moment?
- What do you imagine will be a scenic view you do want to forget?
- Other.

Journal

Do not forget to pack your journal. As we have mentioned throughout the book, taking time to be quiet and collect your thoughts, questions, and concerns is a valuable practice. Your journal can remind you of who you were when this adventure began, what you learned along the way, and capture how you view the adventure in retrospect.

Magnifying Glass

In reflective practice, the magnifying glass symbolizes the process of examining one's thoughts and emotions closely. This metaphor encourages individuals to focus their assumptions about teaching and learning to facilitate a deeper understanding of themselves and promote personal growth. To be critically reflective, we look at our practice—our world—through four lenses: learners' eyes, colleagues' perceptions, personal experience, and theory (Brookfield, 2017 as we described in Chapter 6).

When revisiting these, we encourage you to think about your questions for each of these vantage points. How do you plan to use a magnifying glass in your project?

- Will you use one lens, more than one, or all four?
  - Learners' eyes
  - Colleagues' perceptions
  - Personal experience
  - Theory
- We suggested four ways to engage in practice:
  - *Critical Incident Questionnaire*
  - Exit Slips
  - Plus/Delta Chart
  - Midterm Letter
  - We made our own

Examining our assumptions takes courage and the willingness to be honest with ourselves and our mentoring partner. When we have used items like critical incident questions, we have been delighted to find out what our students like, what they have learned, and what they want to change. Honestly, most of the time, it is easy to accommodate their suggestions or mitigate their frustrations. Understanding the limitations of our own assumptions doesn't have to be painful. A magnifying glass can show the small, sliver-like pain points, which can allow us to remove the sliver and move forward.

A Map

A map is vital to teacher-friend trekking. We like the idea of a topographical (topo) map for two reasons: it is more detailed to help us anticipate challenges, and understanding the scale and grade helps us to prepare ahead of time. A map represents our plan to get from one point to another, our study of the destination, and the possible excitement or challenges along the way. In this section, we will consider the many approaches possible for mid-career teacher-friend mentoring. You will weigh the length and difficulty of each possible destination on the map. In Chapter 9, you will draft your plan with sites to see, sites to avoid, what to pack, what to leave, and, most importantly, why are you going on this adventure?

Metaphorically speaking, review your adventure project and consider the following questions to gauge what you have mapped out.

- Is this a reasonable terrain (not too much uphill climb)?
- Do we want to plan a different trail or area?
- Does the terrain require more than one pair of shoes?
- Will we be walking in the water?
- Is there a cliff?
- Might there be an interesting place to plan on seeing

Micki and Karen's Map and Compass—Writing This Book

We liken a map to our living documents in Dropbox (cloud-based app). We use our shared documents to drop a list of books and topics with fun bullet points into our shared space. We can comment and add to our shared brainstorming list. Because we love gathering ideas and going on tangents, a living document provides us with a place to store random resources or ideas until or if they become useful. We can make a table (We love a good table) to try to see patterns, create a plan, or develop a timeline. We can color code into many categories such as time, topic, or challenge. Our mentoring map comes to life as we trek; individually, we question each other, piggyback off each other's ideas, and grow.

Compass

A compass can be checked at any time on a trek. There are times in October or March when teachers take time to reflect on the school year and find they are not where they expected to be by then. For example, mentoring partners can get stuck talking about frustrations to the exclusion of being creative. At another point, they may be running out of energy and find it hard to solve problems. It is at these points that having a compass is useful. When teacher-friends revisit their mentoring map, they can clearly see where they are in their plans. We can easily lose sight of what is next in our plan, or if a detour is needed, where to go instead of the next planned stop. A compass symbolizes guidance and direction. It often represents the internal or external forces that help navigate life, choices, or challenges.

We like symbolic connections to purpose, choices, and challenges. It is important to remember that the point of a teacher-friend mentor is that we learn together and change together. It is expected, if not mandatory, that while our identity as a teacher remains solid, the pathways and processes need to be adjusted along the way. How will you know when you need to use your compass? We have learned over the years that when everything is falling apart, that is a signal that transformation is happening. The reason life is no longer smooth, and work is difficult, is that we are no longer who we were last year. We have learned, grown, and reflected. We begin to see what no longer fits, that our desires and interests have changed. We have changed. It is time to check our compass.

- Are you on the path to reach your destination?
  - What is your destination?
  - Has it changed?
  - How might you check along the way?
- How are you feeling as you learn and grow?
  - Is your current thinking too tight or too loose?
  - Do you need fresh socks or a change in attitude?
  - Do they stink? Are they soggy? Itchy?

 Sunglasses

Sunglasses represent our perspective, which is our "mental view" and our "capacity to view things in their true relations or relative importance" (Merriam-Webster Dictionary, n.d.). They represent our point of view about teaching and learning. When we pack sunglasses for our trek, we focus on acknowledging our perspectives while being open to learning about others' perspectives.

We resist a new administrative directive, such as a tardy policy. Our reactions can usually be traced back to our views regarding classroom management or student behavior. For example, we value students being on time and in their seats when the bell rings. When administrators do not enforce tardy policies, we may get frustrated because their decisions are not in line with our own views. However, now you can seek out understanding and consider alternative perspectives.

We suggest that mutually beneficial mentoring can foster perspective taking and remind one another to suspend judgment and ask questions. Embracing different perspectives in collaborative work is essential with teachers, administrators, and parents. Teamwork thrives when individuals with varied backgrounds, skills, and experiences come together, but these differences can also lead to misunderstandings if not managed effectively. Rather than simply tolerating other viewpoints, embracing diversity means actively seeking out, valuing, and integrating different perspectives into the team process. Doing so enhances creativity, innovation, and problem-solving.

Fostering an open and productive mentoring relationship starts with valuing each perspective. When people feel heard and respected, they are more engaged and committed to their goals. This not only boosts morale but also strengthens collaboration and performance. Implementing strategies such as open communication, active listening, and encouragement can positively fuel teacher-friend relationships. Ultimately, embracing different perspectives leads to smarter decisions, stronger mentoring teams, and better outcomes.

In the future, consider the following prompts and discuss how you might exhibit adaptability as a mid-career teacher.

- How do we want to remind each other to acknowledge when we are frustrated about a policy or event?
- How can we ask each other questions to open the conversation to multiple perspectives? "Can I ask you some questions?"
- How do we expect the best from one another and steer the conversation to be more productive?

Sunglasses can shade our eyes from the bright sun, focus our attention on an object, and give our eyes rest. In the next section, we will consider journaling to plan our adventure. We will also use a magnifying glass to get a closer look at Brookfield's four assumptions. Discussing our perspectives with a teacher-friend before we leave on an adventure can help us avoid misunderstandings and plan a more satisfying experience.

Sunscreen

Sunscreen is essential to keep them comfortable and protected. In a similar way, setting boundaries and prioritizing work-life balance is essential for mid-career teachers. As teacher-friends, you remind each other to apply and reapply sunscreen, as well as to hold and renegotiate healthy boundaries. We help each other know when to apply sunscreen and when we may be getting too much sun. We remind each other when to say no and when to go home for the purpose of reserving our energy for those we love.

Here are a few ideas to encourage each other to use and reapply boundaries:

- Create a funny code word or phrase—"Don't forget your sunscreen."
- Provide support when there is friction created by those who you say no to after a request.
- Evaluate what work is really important and requires your energy?
- Evaluate what work is not important and how to begin to remove those tasks from your daily routine. For example, we no longer allow students to eat in our classrooms during lunch. This gives us 25 minutes to have an adult conversation and to reset for the afternoon.

Your backpack is packed, and your water bottle is full. Your boot laces are tight and comfortable, while your sunglasses are perched atop your head with the hope for sunny weather. It is time to set out on the adventure that you and your teacher-friend have designed. The map and compass can keep you headed in the right direction. Bringing a camera can bring into focus the change, beauty, and memorable moments.

Conclusion

In this chapter, you planned your trek. You know what you want to learn and how it may impact your practice. Second, you have discussed the best timing for this adventure, when to start, and how long you expect it to take. Lastly, in trekking, packing well is essential to a successful trekking adventure. It is important to know why you are packing each item; do you have a plan to use it? In this chapter, we have provided both reasons to take several items and provided an opportunity for you to think about how each metaphorical item might be used to enhance your goals. In the next chapter, you will be on your way.

References

Brookfield, S. D. (2017). *Becoming a critically reflective teacher* (2nd ed.). Jossey-Bass.

Helmuth, D. (2021). *How to suffer outside. A beginner's guide to hiking and backpacking*. Mountaineers Books.

Merriam-Webster Dictionary. (n.d.). Perspective. In *Merriam-Webster.com dictionary*. Retrieved June 10, 2025 from https://www.merriam-webster.com/dictionary/persepctive

9

On Our Way

This chapter provides opportunities to help you focus and keep the energy of your project moving. This chapter is divided into starting out, a mid-trek check-in, and how to share your trek. Our role in this chapter is to check in with you at each point through questions and prompts. If you get stalled, what strategies might be helpful to refocus? Once you are done, how do you process, evaluate, and share what you have learned?

You are wearing comfortable boots, your backpack is full, your water bottle is filled, and walking poles are at the ready. The adventure has started, and while that sounds easy, it takes a concerted effort. It is easier to talk about something, like going on a trek, than it is to actually go. With that in mind, as you begin to implement this plan, let us remind you why individualized professional development is so effective for mid-career teachers. In previous chapters, we have provided many ideas in which to make a To Do List:

- Find a teacher-friend or decide to trek solo.
- Mull over several possible topics to delve into.
- Decide on a timeline that works for both of your schedules.
- Pack, unpack, and repack your backpacks in anticipation.

Logistics are only half of the challenge when designing individualized professional development. How do we stay engaged in the process when school gets busy and family life ramps up? Teachers are doers; however, we suggest that while trekking teacher-friends maintain a disposition to learn.

DOI: 10.4324/9781003586241-13

Keep Moving

You and your teacher-friend are meeting for the first time to start your mentoring journey. Whether you are reading a book together, taking a class together, or implementing your self-made plan, it is an exciting day. We want to add to the metaphor two items that we feel will help ensure your success: water and walking poles.

Water

Water is essential for hydration; it keeps your mind and body happy. We added water to our list because it needs to be replenished. We imagine that you will find many fun ways to "water" yourselves during this trek. Beverages can quench thirst and re-energize such as water. A beverage can relax us and provide comfort such as a hot cup of tea or coffee. It is important to know when you are dehydrated. The symptoms are getting grumpy, loss of energy, headache, and confusion.

Metaphorically, water represents new ideas and new information, seeking out an alternative perspective than our own.

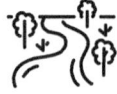

Trail Talk: Water

Water is essential and regulates our mind and body. Discuss with your teacher-friend what you feel like or how you react when you are dehydrated. For example, does it make you tired? How do you feel what you are metaphorically dehydrated? Do you get bored and need fresh ideas to think about or new pedagogies to experiment with in the classroom?

As a teacher-friend, how do you know when you are dehydrated literally and metaphorically?

How might you let your trekking partner know that they may be "dehydrated"?

We know it is important to stay hydrated and to know when we are getting dehydrated ourselves. We need to have a plan to rest, rehydrate, and move forward. As you read through Chapters 1–6, you find hydration stations to provide current research in support of our argument for topics such as dialogue and practice.

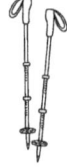

Walking Poles

Walking poles provide stability and support for your body to keep going for the long haul. As trekkers ourselves, we both own walking poles. We like to use them to stay stable on an uneven trail; they support our posture while walking, and they provide an upper body workout. We also like that they are collapsible and can hang off our backpack. Metaphorically, we view walking poles as support. They help us to move forward when the path is difficult. Remember that a trek is much longer than a hike. Walking poles can remind us that this is a long-term plan, and there may be rough trails ahead. Poles extend our inner strength through support, both physically and mentally. They can also represent outer strengths, such as a mentoring relationship. Both signify resilience and progress. When you come to the point when you think you might need to get out your walking poles. For example, in October, the end of the first quarter and parent conferences. Teachers are tired, and parents can be challenged challenging. Questions to consider are: What do you need for support? And how do you support each other?

Trail Talk: Walking Poles

As we discussed above, walking poles provide stability, balance, and support. What do walking poles represent for you? What do you do when you need support?

When do you need to take out your walking poles?

1.
2.
3.

When do poles represent you need to connect with your teacher-friend mentor, or they need to connect (lean) on you?

1.
2.
3.

Water and walking poles support our learning and keep us moving when we are tired. Intellectually, engaged teachers hold onto dispositions that keep them going when teaching becomes challenging.

Dispositions of an Engaged Teacher

As a refresher, let's revisit the four aspects that successful teachers have as successful learners: desire to learn, learnability, learning agility, and transfer of information or skills. We have added this as a refresher because during a busy and/or challenging school year, these dispositions can get lost in the fray.

The first is a *desire to learn*, which describes teachers who are curious, open-minded, and problem-solvers (Berger & Berger, 2018). We previously explained Wink's (2010) concept of learning, unlearning, and relearning, which we adapted to pack, unpack, and repack. Caplan (2013) specifically suggested that teachers with the desire to learn also had the ability to unlearn. This is valuable because the ability to hold complexity and wonder is essential to being open to new learning.

The second is what Henriksen (2018) called *learnability*. This is the desire and ability to learn quickly and adapt new skills to be useful to a teacher in the long-term. He states that teachers' learnability can be identified by assessing three attitudes:

- Intellectual: How motivated or willing are you to learn or understand things better?
- Adventurous: Do you have an intrinsic desire to explore and try new ways of doing things?
- Unconventional: Are you willing to question the status quo?

The third is for teachers to have *learning agility*, which is defined as having the ability to learn quickly and think creatively. These teachers seek out fresh ideas, want feedback from their peers, and explore ways to continually improve both individually and as part of a professional team. High levels of learning agility are characterized by those who are flexible, can manage stress well, and are adaptable to change (Gay & Sims, 2006). Additionally, teachers who are identified to have the desire to learn new pedagogy, skills, and ideas are innovative and reflective (Dalziel, 2018).

Lastly is the ability for teachers to *transfer information or skills from one format to another*. Many professional development workshops are aimed at new teachers. A mid-career teacher may find these presentations redundant or less relevant to their current practice. However, it is a higher level of developmental skill that allows a veteran teacher to transfer and mold professional learning into something useful that can impact their practice (Sasson & Miedijensky, 2023).

These are four important dispositions of being an engaged teacher. Whether you are participating in schoolwide professional development or on your individually designed trek. These dispositions reminded us of Dweck's (2000) growth mindset framework, which is familiar to most teachers.

Growth Mindset

Many of you may use the growth mindset framework in your classroom with students or have learned about it in training. We think it fits for teachers because learning anything new is hard and requires an openness and willingness to consider the possibilities. According to Dweck (2000), those with a growth mindset believe their talents can be developed through hard work, good strategies, and feedback. Conversely, those with a fixed mindset tend to believe that they were born with specific gifts and that those are unchangeable. Dweck suggests that individuals with a growth mindset are more successful because they focus their energy on learning and are less concerned about how they appear to others.

In theory, a growth mindset should play a greater role in a teacher's expectations and practices, as well as for student outcomes. In other words, a growth mindset implies that teachers who hold positive attitudes lean toward learning and improvement. A growth mindset can also impact a teacher's perception of their self-efficacy or effectiveness (Trzesniewski et al., 2021).

So, on our trek, we looked for research on the connection between a growth mindset and teachers. We found a meta-analysis by Bardach et al. (2024) that reviewed and analyzed the findings of 62 research articles about teachers and their growth mindset. The meta-analysis focused on three factors: teacher outcomes, teacher instructional practices, and student outcomes. Their analysis found positive benefits for a growth mindset for teacher self-efficacy, goal setting, and mastery, both for personal and professional contexts.

In other words, a growth mindset is useful for teachers and teacher-friends in terms of setting goals and achieving their goals. It positively impacts individuals both personally and professionally. It is important to note that this meta-analysis did not show a significant impact of teachers' growth mindset on student achievement. However, our connection of growth mindset and teachers' belief that they can influence their goals (efficacy) is at the heart of teacher-friend mentoring and teacher retention.

Journal Prompt: Mindset

Based on the research available and our mutual mentoring foundation, we provide a quick review of growth mindset for you as trekkers.

Growth mindset:

- Embraces challenges
- Persists against obstacles
- Sees effort as necessary
- Learns from criticism
- Is inspired by others' successes

Fixed mindset:

- Avoids challenges
- Gives up easily
- Sees effort as fruitless
- Ignores useful criticism
- Is threatened by others

Take time now to discuss the following prompts and your answers with your teacher-friend.

1. Individually assess your mindset that honestly characterize you.
2. Share your list with your teacher-friend.
3. Discuss the growth mindset skills.
   a. Which skills are you most excited about in your practice?
   b. Which skill are you on the border and why?
   c. Which skill (s) are you in a fixed mindset? Why?
   d. What would help you rethink the assumptions that keep you there?
4. Do you possess the four dispositions of an engaged teacher?
   a. Desire to learn: curious, open-minded, and problem-solver
   b. Learnability: adapt quickly and apply new information
   c. Learning agility: learn quickly, be flexible and creative
   d. Transfer of knowledge or skills to a new situation

By reading this book and/or designing your own trekking experience, you have chosen to give yourself/selves an intellectual boost, professional development, fun, and companionship in a new way. We hope that trekking with a teacher-friend or on your own has literally and metaphorically lightened the load and made space for you to thrive. In the next section, we discuss resting but not quitting. Quitting may not be an option, but resting is a genuine choice.

Journal Prompt: Rest, Repack, Renegotiate

You are about midway through your project plan, maybe halfway through your academic year. It is time to check the map and get an accurate compass reading. It may also be time to have a motivation check; this will help remind you of why you started this project in the first place.

The following list blends individualized teacher professional development and the growth mindset framework to create a checklist that we think is useful mid-trek. Consider using this list to journal, share, and discuss your answers with your teacher-friend.

- Do you have a purpose or goal for your trek?
- Can you identify and discuss any deficits you've found along the way and add new knowledge and skills necessary to be successful?
- Do you view stalls or setbacks as a learning opportunity?
- Is your teacher-friend collaboration working? Are you learning from one another?
- Are you seeing your successes influence success in others such as students and other teachers?

- Are you changing through the process? Are you still passionate about the process?
- Are you taking risks, working through challenges? (Bartz & Kritsonis, 2019).

Congratulate yourselves on completing half of your trek or project. This is a good time to adjust your expectations and possibly consider modifying your destination. In other words, as the year progressed, you may now have different priorities than you did at the beginning of the year. In the next section, we talk about taking a rest rather than abandoning the project or quitting your trek.

Resting Is Not Quitting

One of the best parts about writing this book is learning so much about ideas we didn't have. Rest is one of those areas. I considered rest to be physical or mental, such as taking a nap or not having students in my room at lunchtime. Rest can come in many forms. Skowron (2022) described seven types of rest.

1. *Physical* rest is more than sleep, napping, or sitting. It also includes activities such as yoga or getting a massage.
2. *Mental* rest creates a distance between thoughts and emotions. It is disengaging for a moment from worry and invading thoughts.
3. *Social* rest is about knowing yourself and your needs for interaction. This refers to being an extrovert or an introvert and what type of setting recharges your battery.
4. *Sensory* rest is based on our five senses. It can be a rest from noise and visual input such as computer screens.
5. *Spiritual* rest is when we want to connect with something bigger than ourselves. We can mediate, pray, and volunteer in the community.
6. *Emotional* rest is taking the time to be authentic. Rather than covering up being upset, we walk through the emotion rather than choosing to stuff it down.
7. *Creative* rest is when we take the pressure off to produce art, a hobby, or a project. It is also when we recharge our creative battery by seeking inspiration.

Rest is essential to refuel teachers to do the intense daily work. Remember, teachers make hundreds of decisions a day, just at work. We are passion-driven individuals and know that the cost of this is a time of exhaustion. It is important to identify what kind of rest is needed and when to take time to reset. Many teachers take mental health days and for good reasons. While we are resting, it is also a good time to empty out our backpacks again and repack and refill our water bottles.

Journal Prompt: Rest

What type of rest do you think you need right now?

- How can you plan to get that type of rest? How long do you need to reset?
- How has teacher-friend mentoring supported you so that your endurance in another area has increased?
- How do you support your teacher-friend when he/she needs rest?

As you share your thoughts and journal about rest, you may find it is time to renegotiate the mentoring relationship. You may need rest from each other. If you find yourself in this place, we encourage you not to quit. There is so much to learn about ourselves and from each other, even if it is rough terrain. Here are a few prompts to help you think through what you need, what you want, and what to do next to successfully complete the trek.

Trail Talk

- Get your compass out. Is your trek on course? Are you where you intended to be?
- What have you learned about yourself as a teacher, friend, or leader in your mentoring pair or solo?
- What strengths have you discovered? What strengths have you overused (definition of a weakness)?
- What do you need from mentoring to change so that you can complete your project?

Sharing Your Trek

Your project is complete. You set a goal and a destination, and you have arrived. This trek has made a positive impact on your teaching, it has built intuitive reflective practice muscles, and your efficacy (belief in the capacity to execute behaviors necessary to produce specific performance outcomes) is high.

Sharing your process and outcomes with other teachers is an important next step. It is much like sharing vacation photos with friends after a trip to the Grand Canyon. Trekking and teacher-friend mentoring are unique choices in the professional development arena. You may be the first in your school or district to design self-directed learning, and others can benefit from your courage and tenacity.

Others may want to know what project you chose and how it impacted you personally, your teacher identity, your classroom, and your students. You can share stories of the ups (moments of beauty and courage) and the downs (frustrations and complications). We offer a few ways in which you might share your experience with other mid-career teachers:

1. Share with your professional learning community.
2. Share at a staff meeting.
3. Do a break-out session during professional development days at your school or district level.
4. Do a book study and share your experiences as trekking teacher-friends.
5. Write a short article for a publication such as the *Middle School Journal* (published by the Association for Middle Level Education) the *English Journal* (published by the National Council of Teachers of English), or other professional journals
6. Submit a proposal to present at a local, state, or national conference such as the National Science Teachers Association, National Council for Social Studies, National Council of Teachers of Mathematics, or International Literacy Association.

Conclusion

We are so proud of you for finding a partner, committing to a project or destination, and starting. We also applaud you if you took a solo trek. We encourage you to dig deeper into ideas to find the current research to add to your trail talks and practice. Hydration stations are key to individualized professional development as research grounds what is accurate and moves the conversation forward. We acknowledge that there are parts of the trek that require walking sticks. We get tired or the terrain is steep, and we need support. Trekking partners can help us to identify when a partner needs their sticks, sometimes better than we can as individuals. Teaching is the toggle between passion and exhaustion; it is ok to get support or rest.

This book is predicated on teacher retention. How is it that teachers can mitigate the stress and demands of the job? Resting instead of quitting is an option that is nicely situated inside a community of practice model—if we as teachers begin to influence that conversation. To that end, it is important to share your trek with other teachers who might be ready to individualize their professional development. It is important to share the ups and downs, the triumphs and struggles. All of these are part of any adventure. Sharing with others creates possibilities for others. Adventures change the culture of a school from the inside out and from the teacher to the school level.

References

Bardach, L., Bostwick, K. C. P., Fütterer, T., Kopatz, M., Hobbi, D. M., Klassen, R. M., & Pietschnig, J. (2024). A meta-analysis on teachers' growth mindset. *Educational Psychology Review, 36*(84), 83–118. https://doi.org/10.1007/s10648-024-09925-7

Bartz, D. E., & Kritsonis, W. A. (2019). Micro-credentialing and the individualized professional development approach to learning for teachers. *National Forum Teacher Education Journal, 29*(3), 1–11.

Berger, L. A., & Berger, D. R. (Eds.). (2018). *The talent management handbook* (3rd ed.) McGraw-Hill.

Caplan, J. (2013). *Strategic talent development*. Replika Press.

Dalziel, M. M. (2018). Forecasting employee potential for growth. In L. A. Berger, & D. R. Berger (Eds.), *The talent management handbook* (3rd ed., pp. 129–137). McGraw-Hill.

Dweck, C. (2000). *Self-theories: Their role in motivation, personality, and development*. Psychology Press.

Gay, M., & Sims, D. (2006). *Building tomorrow's talent: A practitioner's guide to talent management and succession planning*. Author House.

Henriksen, T. (2018). Measuring up the skill revolution: Talent assessment in the human age. In L. A. Berger, & D. A. Berger (Eds.), *The talent management handbook* (3rd ed., pp. 138–146). McGraw Hill.

Sasson, I., & Miedijensky, S. (2023). Transfer skills in teacher training programs: The question of assessment. *Professional Development in Education, 49*(2), 243–256.

Skowron, C. (2022, December 21). The 7 kinds of rest you actually need. Social, emotional, sensory, and more. *Psychology Today*. https://www.psychologytoday.com/us/blog/a-different-kind-of-therapy/202212/the-7-kinds-of-rest-you-need-to-actually-feel-rejuvenated

Trzesniewski, K., Yeager, D., Catalán Molina, D., Claro, S., Oberle, C., & Murphy, M. (2021). *Global mindset initiative paper 3: Measuring growth mindset classroom cultures*. https://papers.ssrn.com/sol3/papers.cfm?abstract_id=3911591

Wink, J. (2010). *Critical pedagogy: Notes from the real world*. Pearson.

10

Looking Back, Looking Ahead

Welcome to Chapter 10. You made it to the end of the book and possibly your first trek. In this chapter, we encourage you to *look back* at your trek and *look ahead* to the next trek. As you know, we are big fans of looking at practice to challenge our thinking and make meaning. We think that looking back can also lead you to look ahead to find opportunities for professional growth, those that inspire you or sustain you.

You likely discovered that trekking is not for the faint of heart. You and your teacher-friend shared a vision that professional development could look different in mid-career. You decided to design a project that touched the heart of your practice and your passion. Your self-directed learning took discipline, introspection, accountability, and endurance. This was vastly different than a sit-and-get professional development experience, which only required attendance. Instead, you decided to get out your map, plan a route, pack, and go, knowing that the journey and process were uncertain. One of our favorite authors, Gillie Bolton (2014), expressed:

> *Certain uncertainty is an oxymoron at the heart of reflective practice. ... The only way to get anywhere in reflection and reflexivity is to do it, trusting the journey. We have faith in and respect for ourselves and our abilities to reflect as well as to practice, and generosity and positive regard for fellow travellers such as clients [students] and colleagues. We are open to reassessing our values-in-practice, and formerly strongly held assumptions.*
>
> (p. 197)

DOI: 10.4324/9781003586241-14

Indeed, we felt uncertain many times while writing this book. We had to ask each other a thousand questions, write and rewrite passages to express our ideas in better ways. Our original outline vaguely resembles this final product, but what we valued the most about the process was the journey. In other words, we know more about the research for each topic and how it applies to our individual and collective practice. We know more about the art of teaching and the teeter between passion and exhaustion. We know more about teaching overall.

Looking Back: Our Big Ideas

If we were to post a highlight reel on Instagram from our trek of writing this book, this would be our Top 10 list for trekking with teacher-friends.

1. Teacher-friends make great mutual mentors.
2. Teachers benefit from mentoring that honors their experience and expertise.
3. Reflection is at the heart of purposeful change.
4. Mutual mentoring is purposeful, self-directed, and mutually beneficial.
5. A teacher-friend mentoring approach is professionally meaningful and rewarding.
6. Mutual mentoring elevates and amplifies dialogue, conversation, and good talk.
7. Teaching is a passion-driven profession requiring time and space for recovery and reigniting joy.
8. Mutual mentoring fosters discussion about effective practice.
9. Teacher-friend mentoring can build resiliency and improve self-efficacy.
10. Trekking is a powerful metaphor for self-directed learning for teacher-friends and solo travelers alike.

As you read or reread sections of this book, you may find other key ideas that resonate with you. Your Top 10 list may be like ours; however, we bet it differs. You may even find that your Top 10 lists vary between you and your teacher-friend. You and your trekking partner may look or sound different from how you did when you started. Your teaching and classroom may also look different. More importantly, when you look back on where you have been, you may find yourself being open to more options, more adventures, and more beauty.

The Path Is Made by Walking

The purpose of your trek was to go somewhere new in your personal and professional life. As you may recall, your trek was not a hike; you did not return to where you began. Instead, you ended up somewhere new. Whether you traveled alone or with a teacher-friend, you sought professional growth and personal fulfillment. To characterize this experience, we used a trekking metaphor and highlighted the value of mutual mentorship (Chapter 1).

We used self-directed learning as a framework for individualized professional development (Chapter 2), explaining the process entailed:

- Identifying a learning gap or issue
- Tapping resources to approach closing the gap
- Reflecting on the process and what it reveals
- Applying the new knowledge to address the gap or issue (Brockett & Hiemstra, 2018).

During your first trek, you and your teacher-friend likely experienced the many attributes of self-directed learning elicits: curiosity, flexibility, integrity, and perseverance. We recommend that you adopt self-directed learning as a habit for challenging your own thinking and expanding how you conceptualize teaching. When designing your own professional development, the path is made by walking.

Throughout the book, we introduced you to authors who have contributed to our thinking and practices such as Parker Palmer, Steven Brookfield, Thich Nhat Hanh, and bell hooks. We have read their work individually and together and heard some of them speak at conferences, and even though we do not know them personally, we consider them friends. We summarized their impact on our thinking for the purpose of suggesting that you and your teacher-friend find writers to prompt conversation in your mentoring relationship beyond this trek.

We suggest that reading outside our usual school-related or content-related literature introduces us to new ideas, challenges our thinking, enhances conversations, and can fulfill our need for greater depth in our practice. We agreed that holding complexity:

> *… means that you do not invest your energy in finding the single best solution to the problem you've defined. Instead, you invest your time in understanding, which gives you the chance to find a much larger neighborhood to explore and offers you the opportunity to create a much larger portfolio of solutions.*
>
> (Berger & Johnston, 2015, p. 52)

Teaching is one of the most complex and demanding professions. Many teachers experience stress and burnout; however, we believe that broadening the circle of ideas both personally and professionally can reduce the intense focus on the day-to-day frustrations of teaching.

Taking Stock

As teachers-friends, we want to continuously improve, we want to decide for ourselves, and we now know how to make it happen. In this section, we prompt you to take stock of your trekking adventure.

Because journal writing allows you to take a journey into your interior thoughts, we invite you to reflect on your teacher-friend or solo-trekking adventure. Pause and consider what you learned and how you felt.

Journal Prompt: Trekking Adventure

Open your journal and consider the following reflective questions about your recent trekking adventure.

- What did I learn? How did it feel?
- Would I do it again?
- Am I still a teacher-friend with my trekking partner?
- What do I wish I had known before I left?
- What was the best part?
- What was the most challenging?
- What advice would I give someone before they go?

Next, let's look at what metaphorically carried you (boots) and what you carried (backpack, journal, camera, map and compass, magnifying glass, water bottle, sunglasses, sunscreen) on the trek. Let's begin with your boots.

These well-worn *boots* carried you throughout your trek. You might have slipped them off to allow your toes to breathe or to put on fresh socks. Or perhaps you loosened or tightened the laces for comfort as you traveled. In other words, you made some adjustments along the way so you could reach your destination. As mid-career teachers, your *boots* symbolize your professional and personal fortitude to meet challenges head-on. We suggest that mutual mentoring with a teacher-friend or self-mentoring also requires you to make decisions and adjustments to fit your personal and professional needs.

- What do your boots say about you now?
- Do you need a different type of boot now because you are a different teacher now?
- Are your current boots worn out?

Your *backpack* held all the items you chose to carry on your trekking adventure. You might have overpacked, taking more than you needed to carry. What were you packing that you really did not need? Perhaps, you underpacked and found yourself wishing that you had a few more supplies. Unpacking allows you to evaluate what you truly need (e.g., more water) and what you may want (e.g., less weight) for the next adventure. Dump out your literal or metaphorical backpack and evaluate the contents:

- What is your favorite item?
- What did you not use that surprised you?
- What was invaluable?
- What is now garbage?
- What do you no longer carry around from before you started this adventure?

Among the items inside your backpack, you likely carried your journal, camera, a map and compass, a magnifying glass, and a water bottle.

Your *camera* captured metaphorical photographs from a single moment or situation. The images allowed you to revisit a situation, notice the details, and fill in the blanks about what happened before and after the event.

- What type of camera did you carry?
- Did you use the camera on your phone to document your trek?
- When looking back at your photos, where did you find yourself (e.g., on top of a mountain, at the trailhead, soaking your feet in the stream)?
- What other images did you wish to capture?

Your *journal* represented teacher reflection. Keeping a journal allows you to record your inner thoughts.

- What type of notes were important to write down and keep track of during your adventure?
- Was there a recognizable theme?
- Looking back, is there a theme you wish you had documented from the beginning?

You used a *map* and a *compass*, too. You referred to your *map* to plan the trek, look at the terrain, assess the distance, and determine a timeline. You pulled out a compass from time to time to verify that you were on the right path.

- Did the trek meet your expectations?
- Was it as easy to use the map (plan)?
- Did the trek go as planned, or was it harder than expected?
- How did you use a compass during this trek to make sure you were on track or to make changes to the plan?

The *magnifying glass* allowed you to examine your own assumptions about teaching using Brookfield's (1998) four lenses: autobiographical, learners' eyes, colleagues' perceptions, and theoretical. Peering through the magnifying glass was a personal choice to consider your teaching practice.

- What did you notice when reflecting on your practice?
- How did your personal experiences shape your trek?
- Did your assumptions about student learning help or impede your journey?
- How did your teacher-friend serve as a mirror for you along the path?
- What theory, if any, validated your own thoughts and assumptions about teaching?

You refilled your *water bottle* at each *hydration station*. Throughout the book, we presented recent research and salient theories about numerous ideas pertaining to teaching, professional development, and personal growth. You might have "collected" stickers (ideas) from each hydration station. The purpose of these stations was to add recent research and relevant theories into the conversation.

- Dialogue, Conversation, and Good Talk (Chapter 3)
- Practice: Going Deeper and Moving Forward (Chapter 4)
- Teacher Well-Being and Resiliency (Chapter 5)
- Packing, Unpacking, and Repacking (Chapter 6)
- Teaching, Passion, and Trekking (Chapter 7)

Your *sunglasses* allow you to see the world differently. You put them on and slipped them off whenever the light or conditions changed. Wearing your sunglasses represented a purposeful and practice choice to change your perspective.

- How did a change in perspective influence your practice?
- Did a change in perspective prompt a change in your goals?
- When was it most helpful to consider another perspective?

 You not only carried *sunscreen*, but you applied it liberally to preserve the health of your skin. It formed a boundary between your skin and the harmful rays of the sun. Like sunscreen protects skin, you have learned to set boundaries and hold reasonable expectations for yourself.

- What boundaries did you set for your trekking adventure?
- Did you remind yourself and your teacher-friend about the importance and value of setting boundaries for yourselves?
- What did you learn about your personal and professional boundaries?

We believe that looking back (reflection) on your trekking adventure holds tremendous power. It prompts you to consider where you have been and how you got there and uncovered new ground. Looking back can also help prepare us to look ahead.

Looking Ahead: Our Beliefs

First, we consider the original dilemma of this book. How do teachers stay in a profession they are passionate about? While we know passion can wane, we are certain that it can also be renewed.

The Original Dilemma: Should I Stay or Should I Go?

Perhaps you have heard the song, *Should I Stay or Should I Go*, released by the English punk rock band, The Clash (1982). Or perhaps you heard it in the 1990s, when the song reappeared in a Levi's commercial. While the band claimed the song was just a song, some assigned meaning to the lyrics (a breakup). Today, some teachers, including mid-career teachers, are asking the same question. Should I stay or should I go?

As you likely recall, we shared why teachers are deciding to "go." We cited research about the reasons teachers reported for leaving the profession (e.g., burnout or exhaustion, heavy workload, low pay, large class size, disruptive student behavior). Yet, other teachers are not going. In fact, we also found recent research about teachers who are deciding to "stay."

Why have teachers decided to stay in the teaching profession? Based on her study of mid-career teachers, Maynard (2024) identified three overarching reasons:

1. Relationships with students and staff
2. Desire to teach
3. Teacher appreciation

First, *relationships with students and staff* contributed significantly to teachers' decisions to remain in the game. Relationships with students were the reason most mid-career teachers gave for staying in the teaching profession. They also wanted to collaborate with and support peer teachers and share decision-making with school leaders. Second, teachers possessed a *desire to teach*. They wanted to make a difference in students' lives, enjoy teaching, and believe they are good at their work. Third, *teacher appreciation* was important for mid-career teachers. They felt valued, had opportunities for professional development, and enjoyed job security.

Maynard's (2024) findings resonated with us as well. We enjoy positive relationships with most of our fellow teachers and most of our students. Building relationships and receiving positive feedback from our students and colleagues fills our hearts and keeps us seeking adventure. We hold the art of teaching at the forefront of our minds and seek ways to be creative and build our repertoire. Because we develop our practice and grow over time, we want professional development options that are personally meaningful and validate us as teachers.

We assert that our teacher-friend mentoring approach aligns with Maynard's findings. Whether you are designing your own professional development plan or completing your trek, we hope the mutual mentoring approach is meaningful and expands your sense of agency.

Your personal and professional agency, in turn, reveals your feeling of being in control of your life and influences how you think and act. Agency, in a teacher-friend mentoring relationship or self-mentoring, relates to your belief in your ability to face the multitude and complex challenges of teaching in today's classrooms and schools. Let's take a brief look at beliefs.

Beliefs about Teaching

Beliefs are what we have faith in. These are the ideas we accept or consider to be true; they can also be our opinions. We find it valuable to engage in good talk (see Chapter 3) about our beliefs. Because we think you may find it valuable as well, we invite you to pause and develop a set of your belief statements.

What Do You Believe?

To get you started, consider your beliefs about teaching, relationships, mentoring, and taking risks.

Journal Prompt: Beliefs
You can compose a list of beliefs with your teacher-friend. Or you can write your own list of beliefs. Feel free to note these in your journal.

Teacher-Friend Trekkers	Solo Trekker
We believe …	I believe

You can revisit your list of beliefs from time to time. When revisiting your list, you may find yourself revising your list by modifying, adding, or even discarding belief statements.

What Do We Believe?
We find ourselves thinking about our beliefs all the time. We rewrite and refine our list of belief statements from time to time. The following is our most recent iteration about what we believe about teaching, relationships, mentoring, and taking risks.

We believe …

- teaching is an art;
- in the power of relationships;
- teacher-friends make a difference;
- mentoring matters across the life span;
- mutual mentoring must be mutually beneficial;
- mid-career teachers can design their own professional development; and
- teachers contribute to communities of practice that positively influence a school's culture.

Conclusion

Mid-career teachers are a treasure to the profession. They bring stability, history, skills, and strength to a school community. As many teachers are leaving the profession due to a myriad of frustrations, you have chosen to stay a while longer. Our final thoughts for you are that with wisdom comes grace. We view grace as a muscle that grows with use. We consider critical thinking about our practice and grace being different sides of the same coin. You cannot have one without the other.

As we wrote this book, we also read *How to Suffer Outside: A Beginner's Guide to Hiking and Backpacking* (Helmuth, 2021) to help guide the development and implementation of the trekking metaphor. Helmuth (2021) shared these reflections on hiking and backpacking: "But, luckily, some of the effects lasted longer: gratitude for things I once consider normal, patience with uncertainty, and a sense of humor about the subjective way we live, survive, and take care of ourselves" (p. 218). Helmuth's words captured an overarching idea about the value of trekking with teacher-friends. Mentoring is mutually beneficial when we show up as our authentic selves, and we are gentle with ourselves and others. Our treks require gratitude, patience, and humor. We enjoy trekking and writing for you, and we hope that your trek renews your passion for teaching and energy for adventure.

References

Berger, J. G., & Johnston, K. (2015). *Simple habits for complex times: Powerful practices for leaders.* Stanford Business Books.

Bolton, G. (2014). *Reflective practice: Writing and professional development* (4th ed.). SAGE Publications Ltd.

Brockett, R. G., & Hiemstra, R. (2018). *Self-direction in adult learning: Perspectives on theory, research and practice* (eBook). Routledge. https://doi.org/10.4324/9780429457319

Brookfield, S. (1998). Critically reflective practice. *Journal of Continuing Education in the Health Professions, 18*(4), 197–205. https://doi.org/10.1002/chp.1340180402

Helmuth, D. (2021). *How to suffer outside: A beginner's guide to hiking and backpacking.* Mountaineers Books.

Maynard, K. (2024). *What are the reasons mid-career teachers continue teaching?* [Thesis, University of Illinois at Urbana-Champaign]. hhttps://www.ideals.illinois.edu/items/132613

The Clash. (1982). Should I stay or should I go [Song]. On *Combat Rock*. Epic.

Epilogue
Micki and Karen's Trekking Adventure

Writing this book has been quite an adventure. Over the last year, we traveled a long path using the same trekking approach we recommend in this book. Now we find:

- Our boots supported our work and remained as comfortable as ever.
- Our backpacks returned full of more ideas and souvenirs to remind us of all the places we have been.
- Our journal holds insightful reflections, many notes, lots of questions, lovely sketches, and rich memories.
- Our camera captured photos of important moments and places we visited—ones we cherished and did not want to forget.
- Our water bottles refreshed and renewed our minds and bodies whenever we got tired.
- The map (our book outline) is full of handwritten notes, scratched-out text, ideas from our scholar friends, watermarks, wrinkles from being crowded in our backpacks, and rips from overuse.
- Our sunglasses allowed us to see a variety of ideas and each other more clearly as our perspectives broadened and changed.
- We are out of sunscreen, so now it is time for a new tube for our next adventure.
- We appreciated having our walking poles for the time when this project seemed too steep or too rocky. We even relied on our poles while going downhill to finish this project so as not to slip.

In hindsight, writing this book was truly an inspiring trek. We have reached our destination, which is a new and beautiful place. Professionally, we are smarter, and personally we are stronger and wiser from this walk.

Our trekking metaphor captured the essence of mutual mentoring and work-life friendships that flourish when teachers support each other.

For Product Safety Concerns and Information please contact our EU
representative GPSR@taylorandfrancis.com
Taylor & Francis Verlag GmbH, Kaufingerstraße 24, 80331 München, Germany